BIG BOOK OF

BALLADS

W9-BHN-763

ISBN 0-634-00468-9

HAL•LEONARD® CORPORATION

7777 W. BLUEMOUND RD. P.O. BOX 13819 MILWAUKEE, WI 53213

Visit Hal Leonard Online at
www.halleonard.com

CONTENTS

All by Myself

Music by SERGEI RACHMANINOFF
Words and Additional Music by ERIC CARMEN

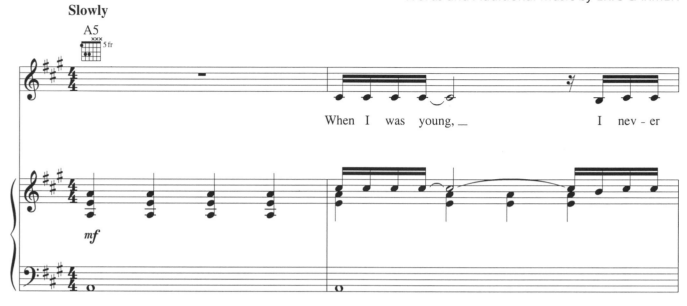

When I was young, ___ I nev - er

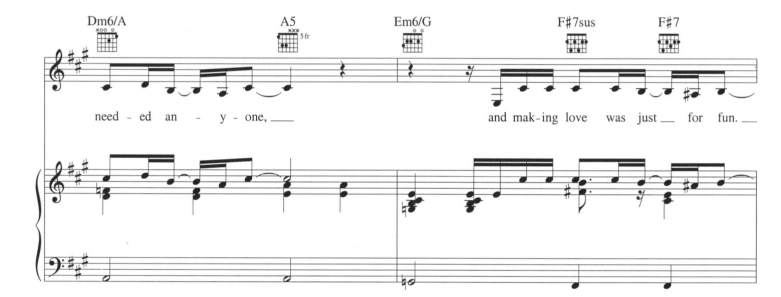

need - ed an - y - one, ___ and mak-ing love was just ___ for fun. ___

___ Those days ___ are gone. ___

Tempo I

When I was young, __ I nev-er need-ed an - y - one, __ and mak-ing love was just __ for fun. __ Those days __ are gone. __ All by __ my - self, __

molto rit.

a tempo

8

And I Love You So

Words and Music by
DON McLEAN

Almost Paradise
Love Theme from the Paramount Motion Picture FOOTLOOSE

Words by DEAN PITCHFORD
Music by ERIC CARMEN

(Male:) I thought that dreams_ be - longed _ to
(Male:) It seems like per - fect love's _ so

oth - er men, _ 'cause each time I _ got close _ they'd
hard to find. _ I'd al - most giv - en up. _ You

fall a - part _ a - gain. _ (Female:) I feared my heart _ would beat in
must have read _ my mind. _ (Female:) And all these dreams_ I saved for a

Beauty and the Beast

from Walt Disney's BEAUTY AND THE BEAST
As Performed by Celine Dion and Peabo Bryson

Lyrics by HOWARD ASHMAN
Music by ALAN MENKEN

Ben

Words by DON BLACK
Music by WALTER SCHARF

Moderately

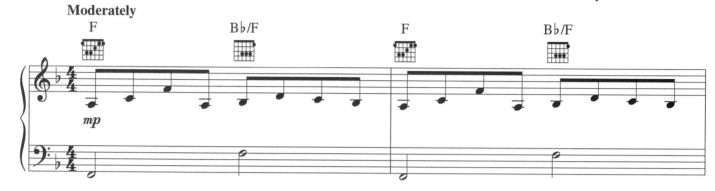

Ben, the two of us need look no more. We both found what we were

look-ing for. With a friend to call my own, I'll nev-er be a-

Candle in the Wind

Music by ELTON JOHN
Words by BERNIE TAUPIN

Good-bye Nor - ma Jean, _____ though I nev - er
Lone - li - ness _ was tough, _____ the tough - est role

knew you _ at all you had the grace to hold your-self _ while
you ev - er played. Hol - ly-wood cre - at - ed a su - per - star _ and

those a - round _ you crawled. _ They crawled out of the
pain was the price you paid. _ E - ven when you

rain set in. ___ I would have liked ___ to have known

you, but I was just ___ a kid. Your can - dle burned ___ out

long be - fore ___ your leg - end ev - er did. ___

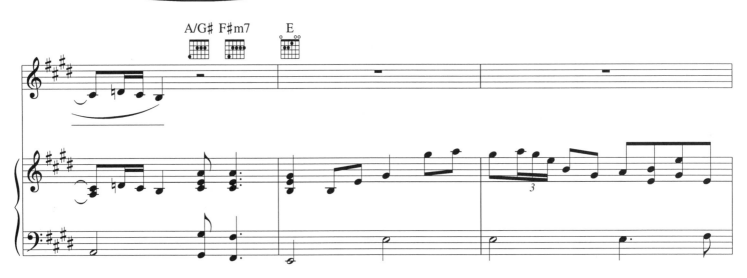

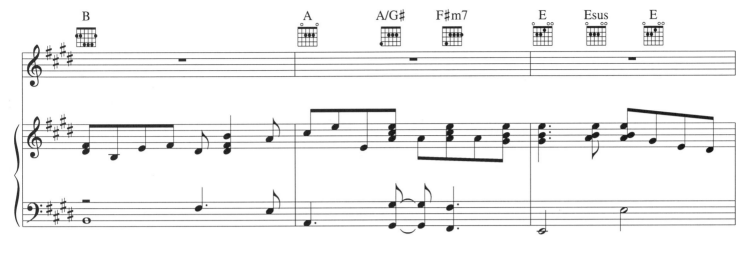

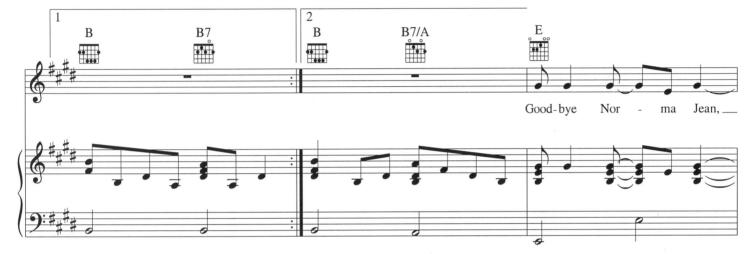

Good-bye Nor - ma Jean, ___

___ though I nev - er knew you ___ at all you had the grace to

hold your-self ___ while those a - round ___ you crawled. ___

Colors of the Wind
from Walt Disney's POCAHONTAS
As Performed by Vanessa Williams

Music by ALAN MENKEN
Lyrics by STEPHEN SCHWARTZ

You think you own what-ev-er land you
think the on - ly peo-ple who are

land on;   the earth   is just a dead thing you can claim;   but
peo - ple   are the peo - ple _ who look and think like you,   but

Change the World

featured on the Motion Picture Soundtrack PHENOMENON

Words and Music by GORDON KENNEDY,
TOMMY SIMS and WAYNE KIRKPATRICK

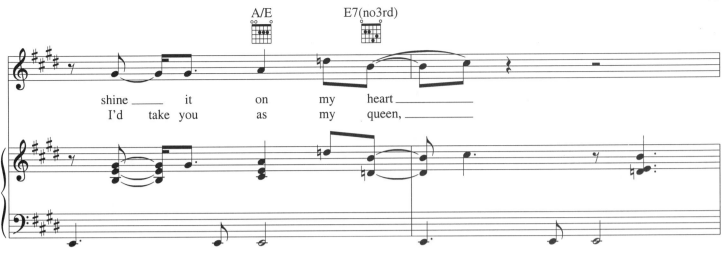

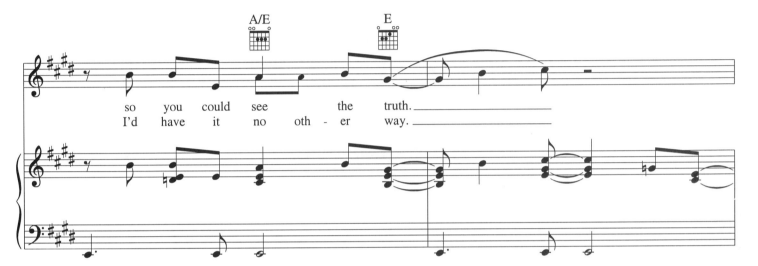

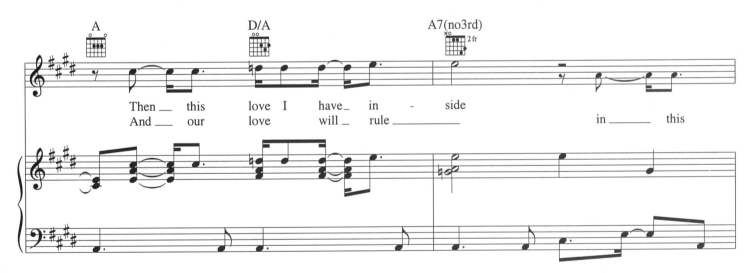

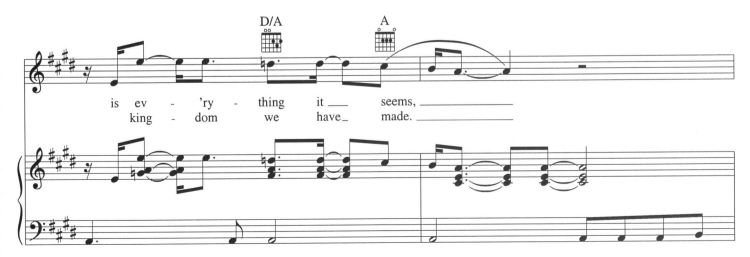

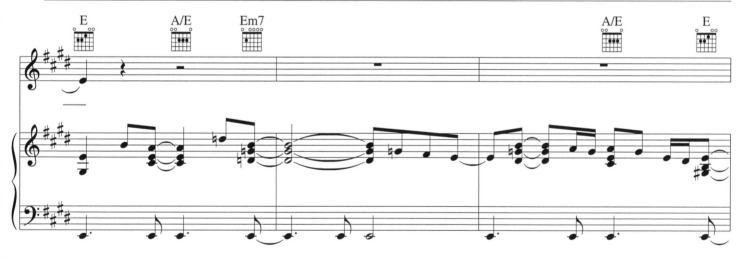

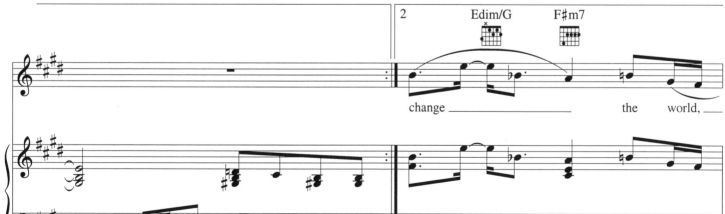

ba - by,__ if I__ could__ change _____

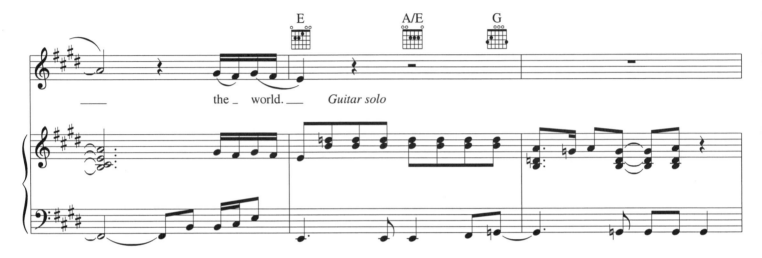

the __ world. __ *Guitar solo*

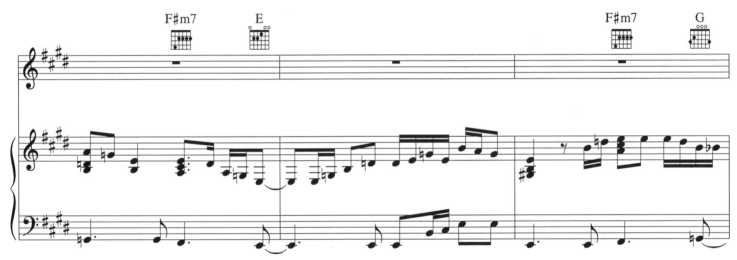

D.S. al Coda

Solo ends I could

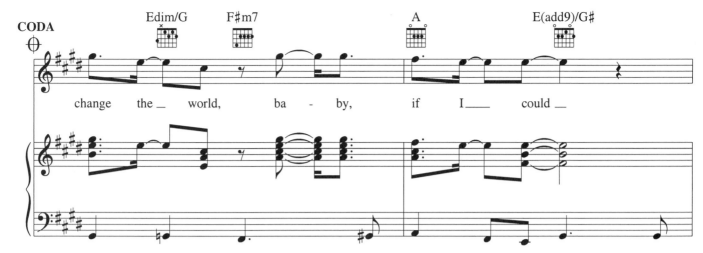

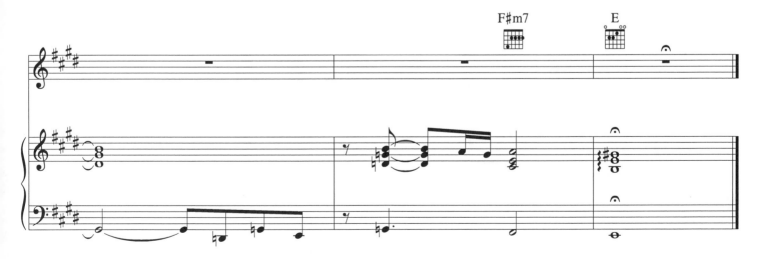

(They Long to Be)
Close to You

Lyric by HAL DAVID
Music by BURT BACHARACH

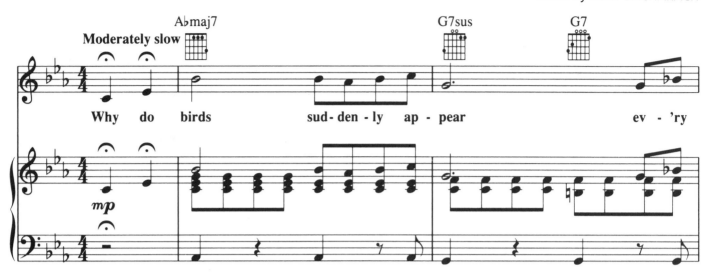

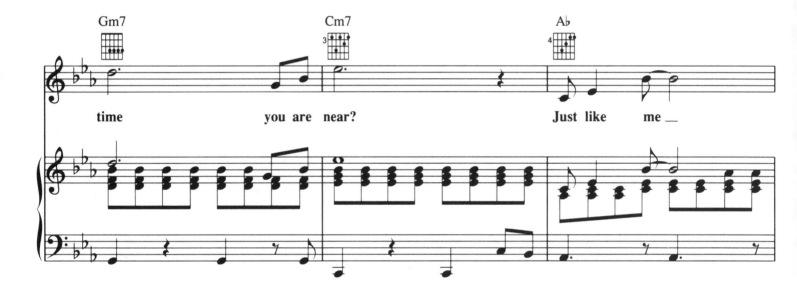

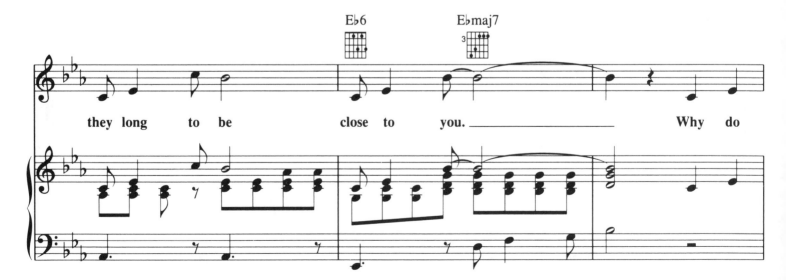

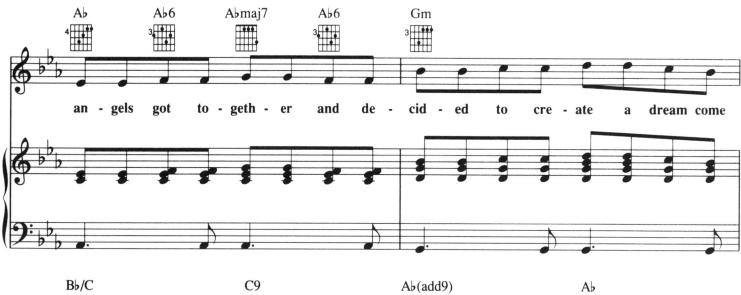

an - gels got to - geth - er and de - cid - ed to cre - ate a dream come

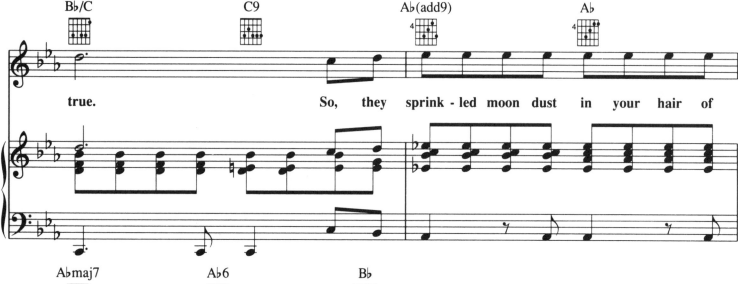

true. So, they sprink - led moon dust in your hair of

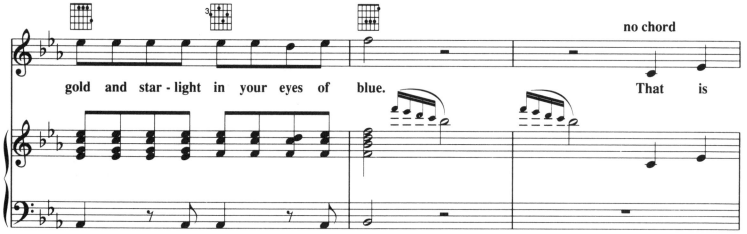

gold and star - light in your eyes of blue. That is

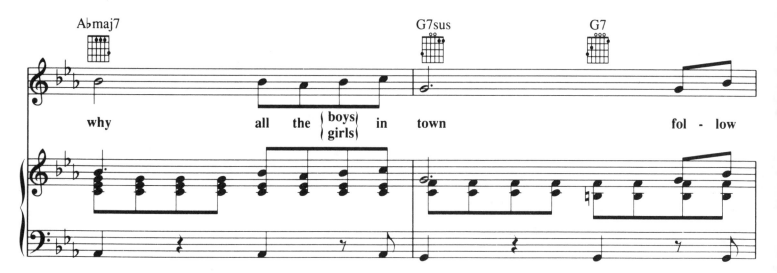

why all the {boys} {girls} in town fol - low

Could It Be Magic

Words and Music by ADRIENNE ANDERSON
and BARRY MANILOW

Spir-it move __ me ev-'ry time I'm near __ you, whirl-ing like __ a cy-
La-dy, take __ me high up-on __ a hill - side, high up where __ the stal-

- clone in my mind.
- lion meets the sun.

Sweet Me - lis -
I could love __

Dsus D E♭maj7 Dm7 E♭maj7

- sa, an - gel of ___ my life - time, an - swer to ___ all an -
___ you; build - ing my world a - round ___ you, nev - er leave ___ you till ___

D7sus Dm7 Gsus(add2) G G7/F Cm/E♭ G7/D

- swers I can find; ba - by, I love ___ you.
___ my life is done. Ba - by, I love ___ you.

Cm A♭/C Bm7 G/B B♭maj7 B♭6

(1., 3.) Come, come, come in - to ___ my ___ arms.
(2., 4.) Now, now, now and hold ___ on ___ fast.

Am7 A♭7 G **To Coda** ⊕

Let me know ___ the won - der of all ___ of you. ___
Could this be ___ the mag - ic at last? _____

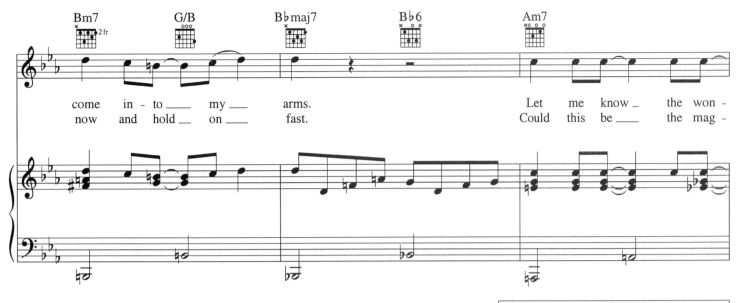

come in-to ___ my ___ arms.
now and hold ___ on ___ fast.
Let me know ___ the won-
Could this be ___ the mag-

- der   of   all ___ of   you. ___
- ic   at   last? _____
Ba - by, I   want ___ you.
Could it be mag - ic?

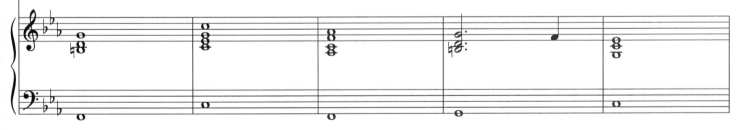

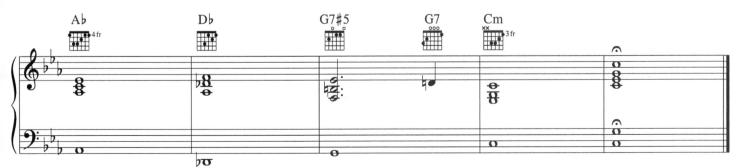

Crazy

Words and Music by
WILLIE NELSON

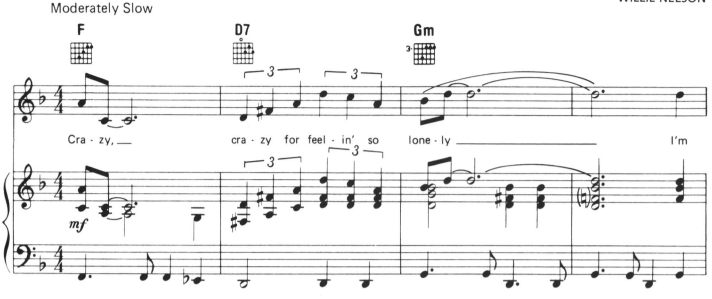

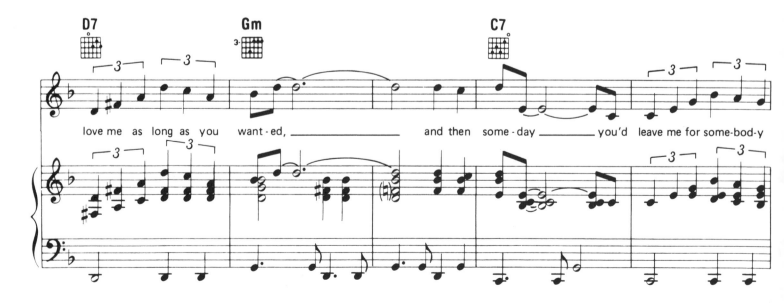

Easy

Words and Music by
LIONEL RICHIE

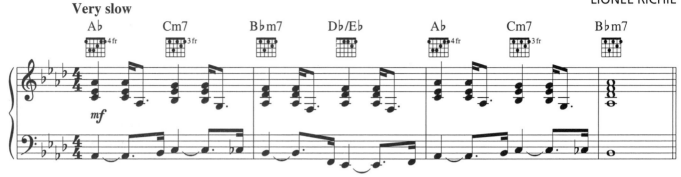

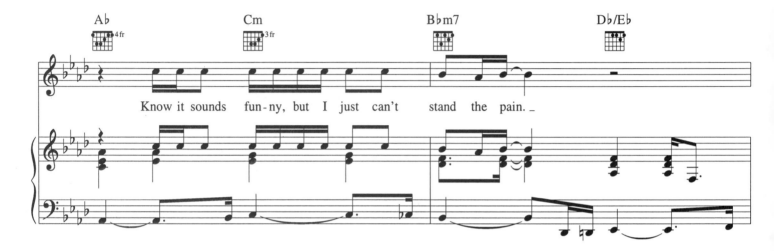

Know it sounds fun-ny, but I just can't stand the pain.

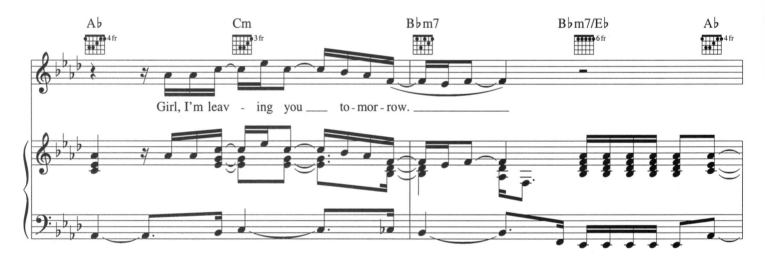

Girl, I'm leav-ing you ___ to-mor-row. ___

Seems to me, ___ girl, you know I've done all ___ I can.

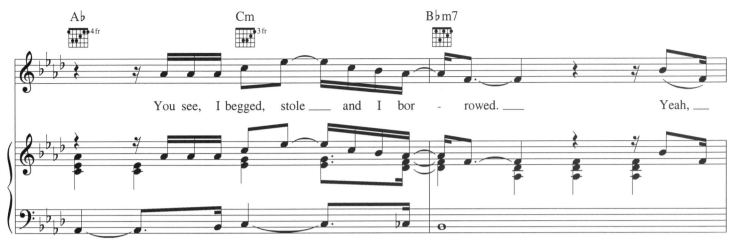

You see, I begged, stole ___ and I bor - rowed. ___ Yeah, ___

ooh. That's why I'm eas - y, ___
(Ah) ___

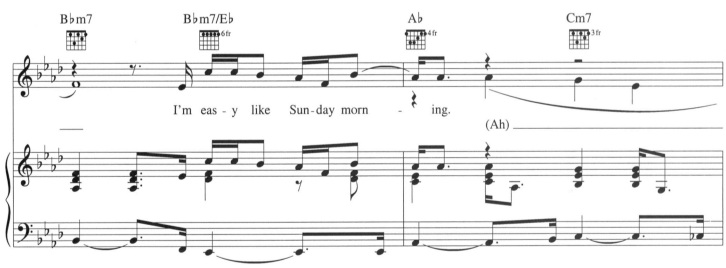

I'm eas - y like Sun-day morn - ing.
(Ah) ___

That's why I'm eas - y. ___

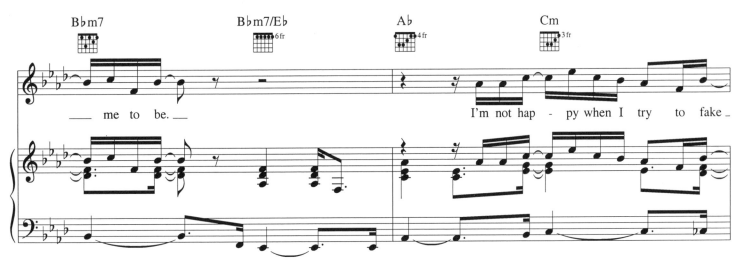

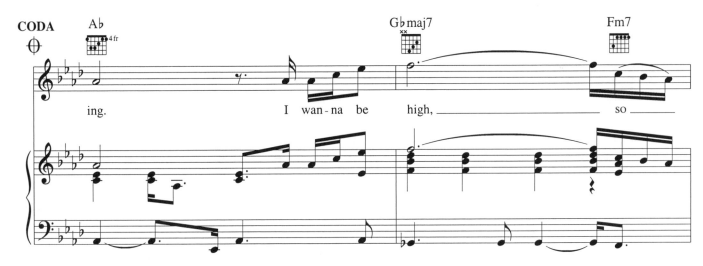

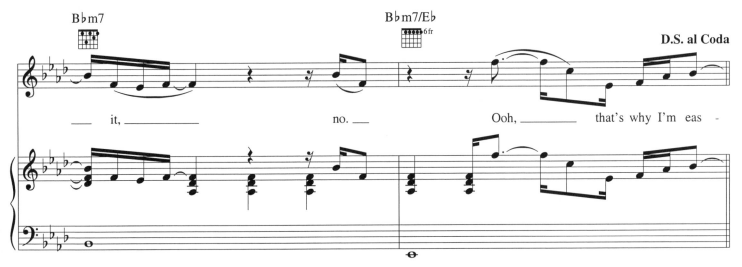

I wan-na be free, ____ just ____

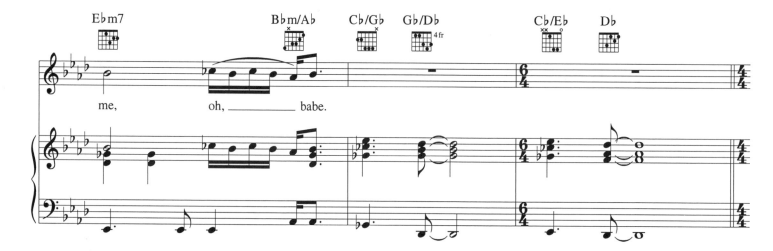

me, oh, _____ babe.

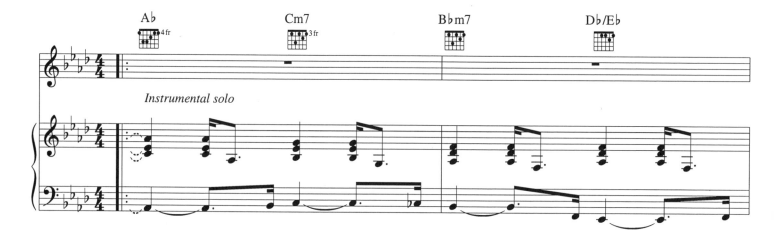

Instrumental solo

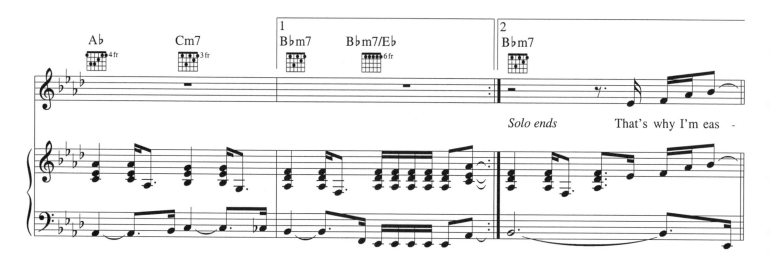

Solo ends   That's why I'm eas -

Endless Love

from ENDLESS LOVE

Words and Music by
LIONEL RICHIE

Moderately slow

My love, ___ there's on - ly you in my life, ___
Two hearts, ___ two hearts that beat as ___ one; ___

the on - ly thing that's right. ___ My
our lives have just be - gun. ___ For -

first ___ love, ___ you're ev - 'ry breath that I take, ___
ev - er, ___ I'll hold you close in my arms, ___

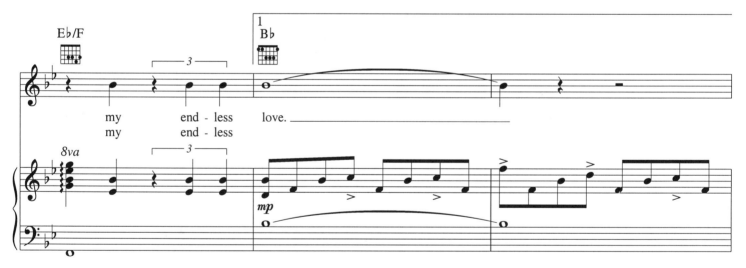

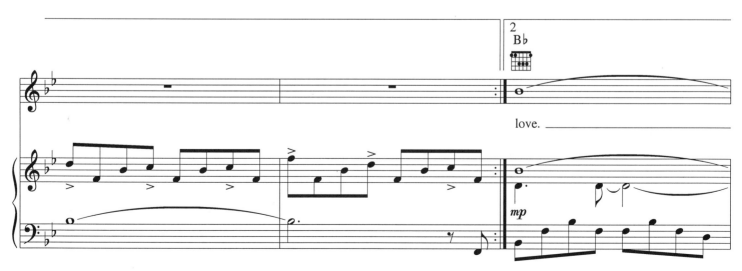

Oh, _____ and _____ love, _____

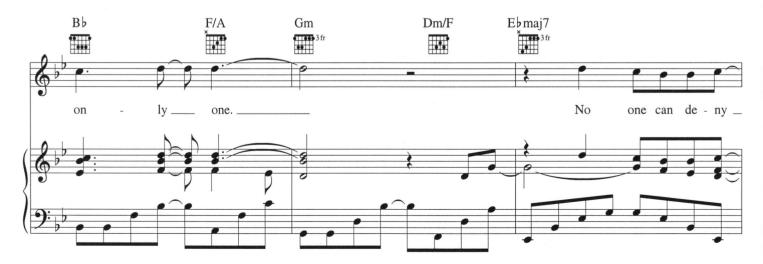

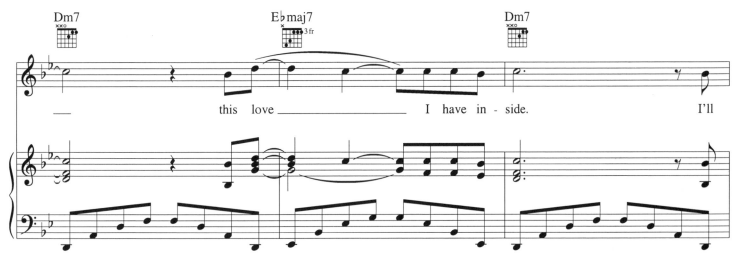

this love _____ I have in - side. I'll

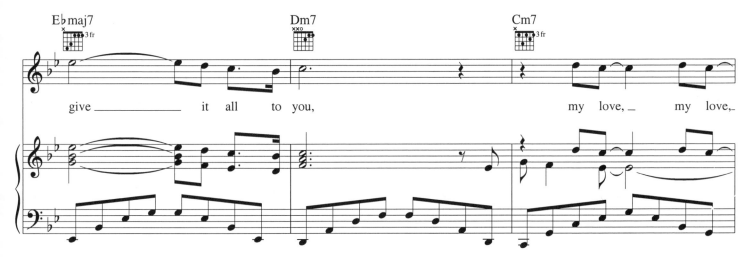

give _____ it all to you, my love, ___ my love, ___

___ my end - less love.

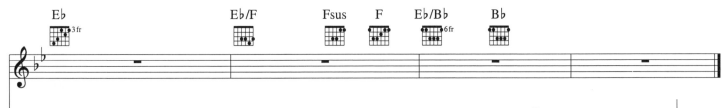

Fields of Gold

Written and Composed by
STING

The First Time Ever I Saw Your Face

Words and Music by
EWAN MacCOLL

The first time
The first time
The first time

ev-er I
ev-er I
ev-er I

saw your face,
kissed your mouth,
lay with you

I thought the sun
I felt the earth
and felt your heart

rose in your eyes,
move in my hand,
so close to mine,

Go the Distance

from Walt Disney Pictures' HERCULES
As Performed by Michael Bolton

Music by ALAN MENKEN
Lyrics by DAVID ZIPPEL

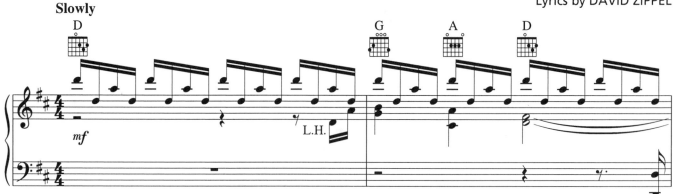

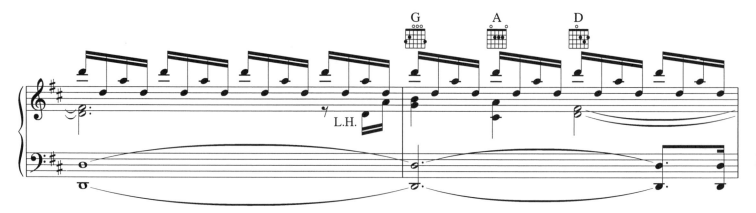

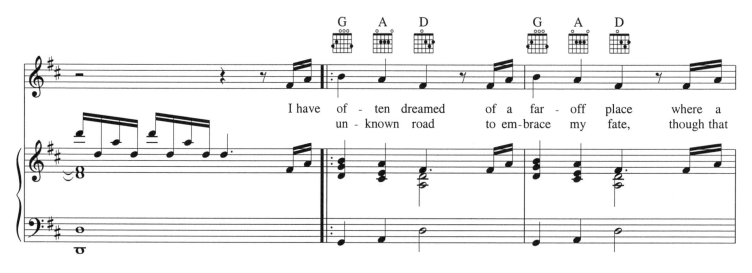

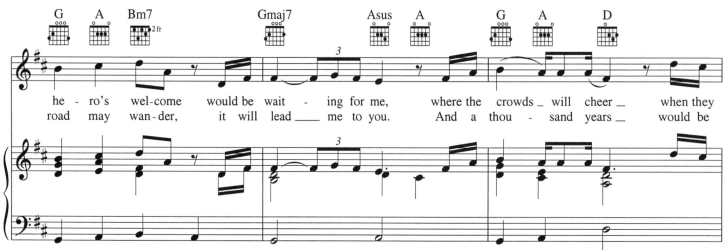

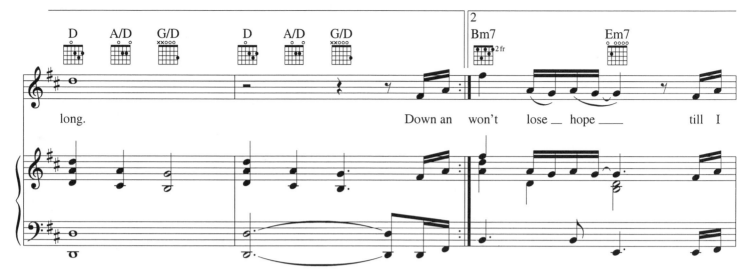

long.　Down an won't lose ___ hope ___ till I

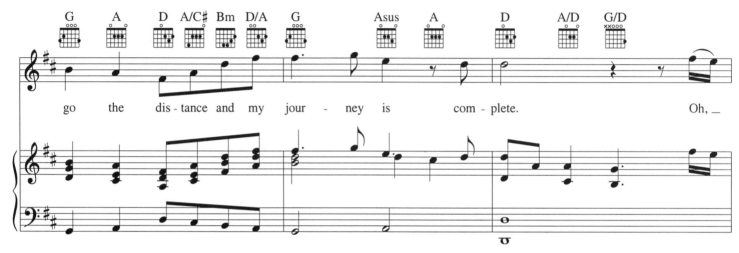

go the dis-tance and my jour-ney is com-plete.　Oh, ___

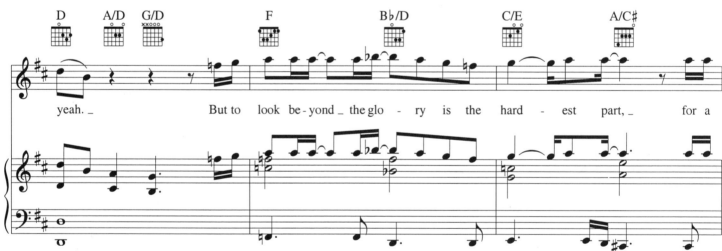

yeah. ___　But to look be-yond ___ the glo-ry is the hard-est part, ___ for a

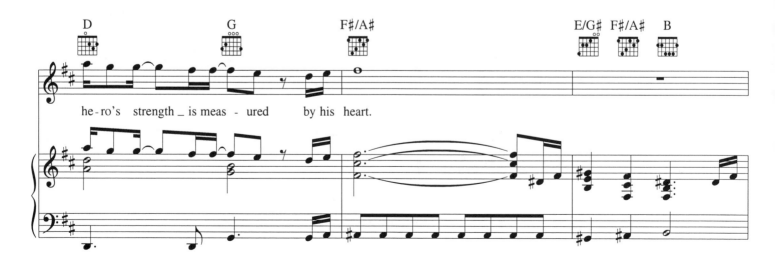

he-ro's strength ___ is meas-ured　by his heart.

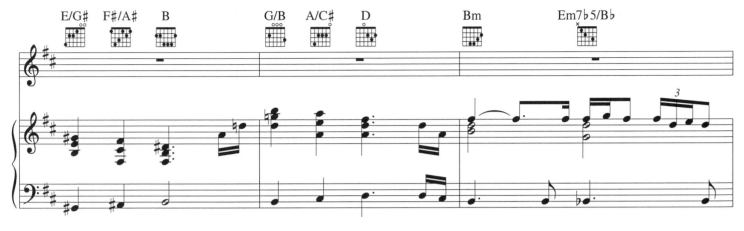

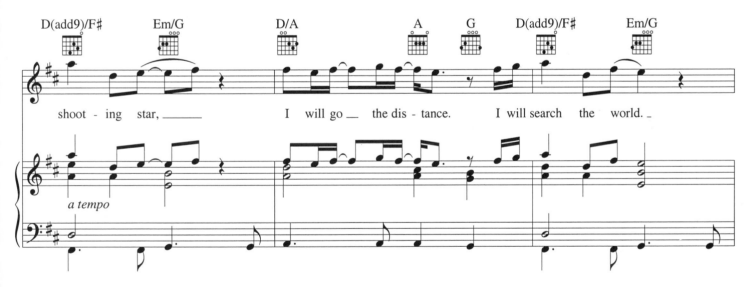

shoot - ing star, _____ I will go _ the dis - tance. I will search the world. _

I will face _ its harms. I _____ don't care how far. _____ I can go the dis - tance till I

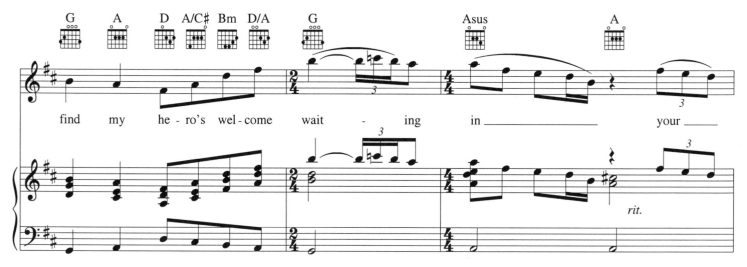

find my he-ro's wel-come wait - ing in _____ your _____

Broadly

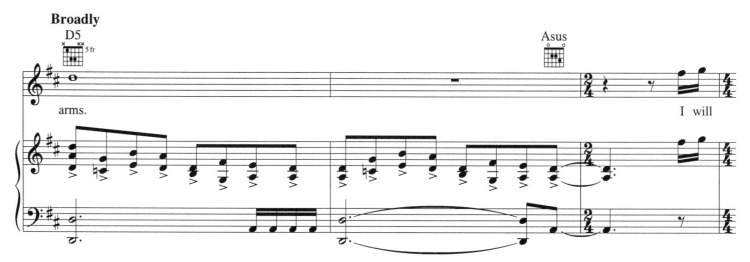

arms. I will

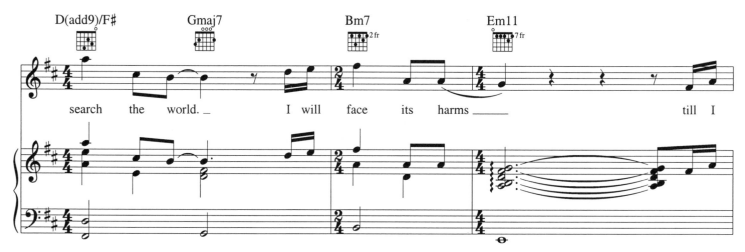

search the world. ___ I will face its harms _____ till I

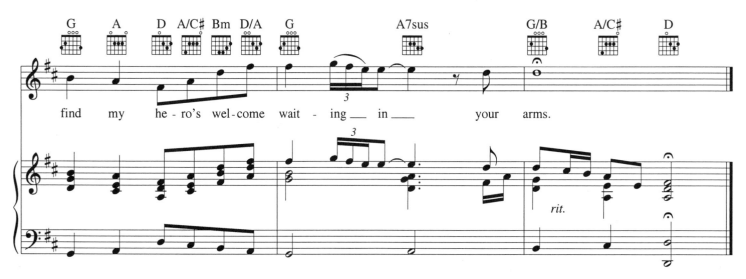

find my he-ro's wel-come wait - ing ___ in ___ your arms.

Goodbye Yellow Brick Road

Words and Music by ELTON JOHN
and BERNIE TAUPIN

Moderately slow, in 2

When are you gon-na come down   When are you going to land___
What do you think you'll do then   I bet that-'ll shoot down___ your plane___

___ I should have stayed___ on the farm___   Should have list-ened___ to my___ old man___
It-'ll take you a cou-ple of vod-ka and ton-ics to set you on your feet a-gain___

___ You know you can't hold___ me for-ev-er___   I did-n't sign up___ with you___
May-be you'll get___ a re-place-ment___ there's plen-ty like me to be found___

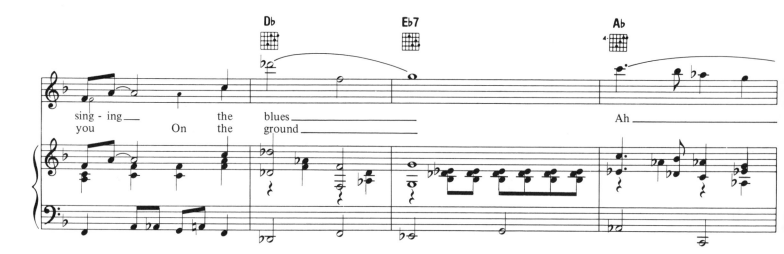

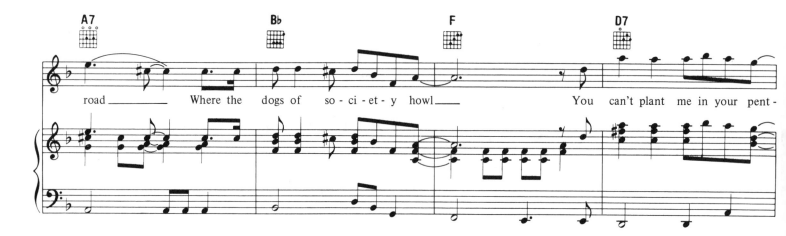

Grow Old With Me

Words and Music by
JOHN LENNON

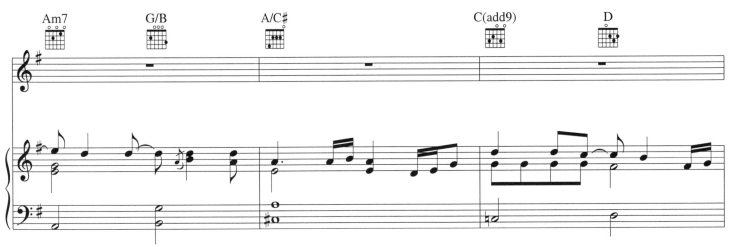

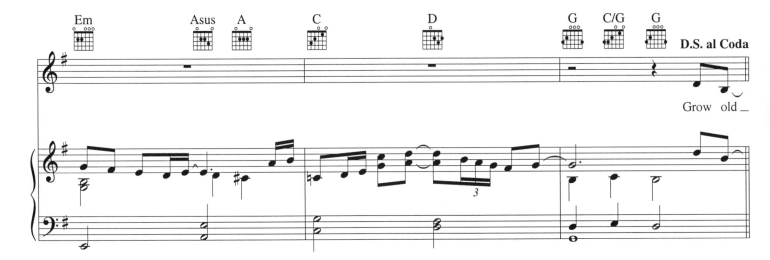

Grow old

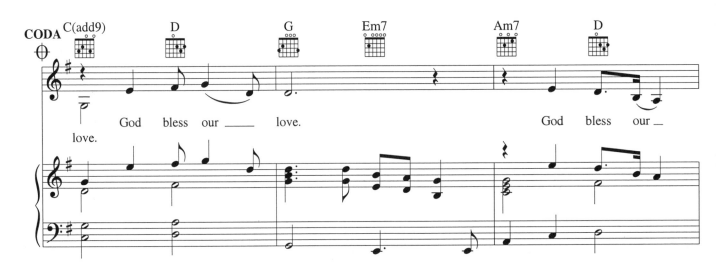

God bless our _____ love.

love.

God bless our _

love.

Have I Told You Lately

Words and Music by
VAN MORRISON

Slowly, with expression

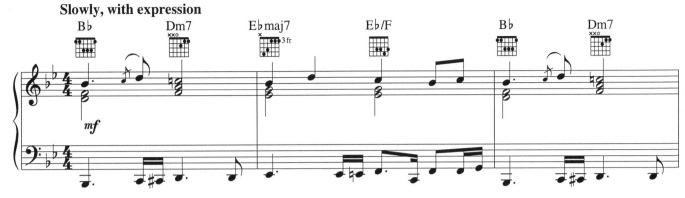

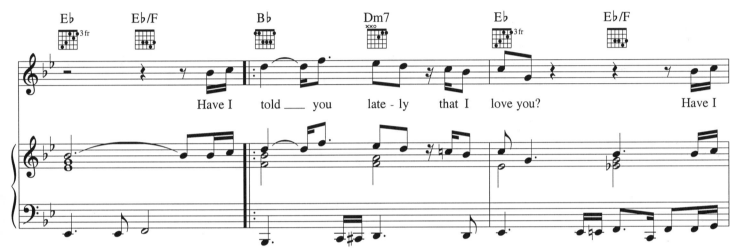

Have I told ___ you late - ly that I love you? Have I

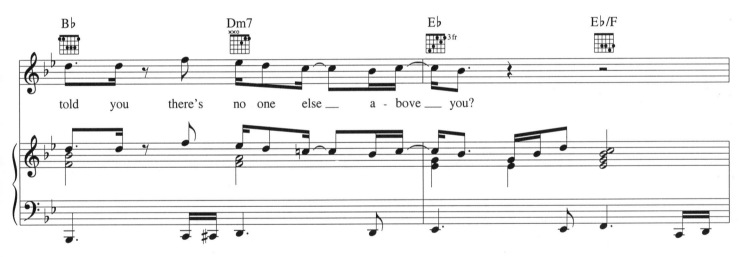

told you there's no one else ___ a - bove ___ you?

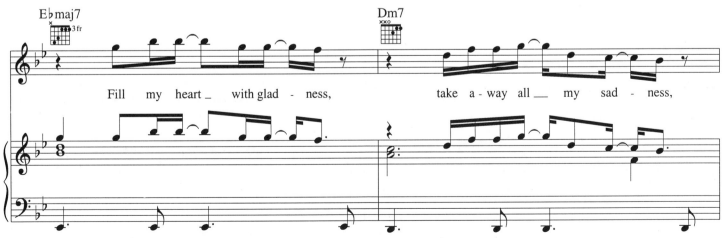

Fill my heart ___ with glad - ness, take a - way all ___ my sad - ness,

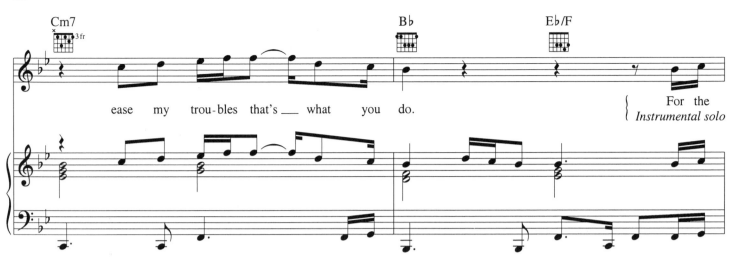

ease my trou-bles that's __ what you do.

For the
Instrumental solo

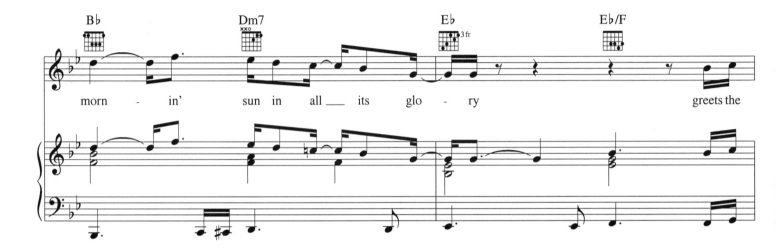

morn - in' sun in all __ its glo - ry

greets the

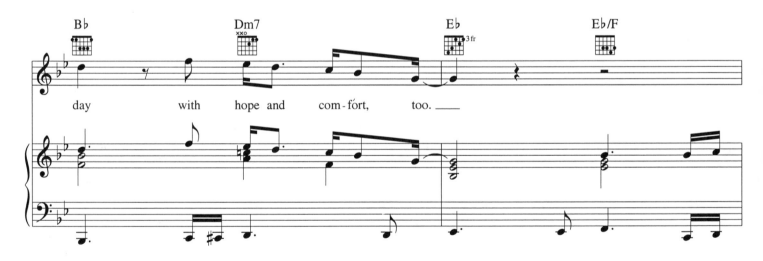

day with hope and com-fort, too. __

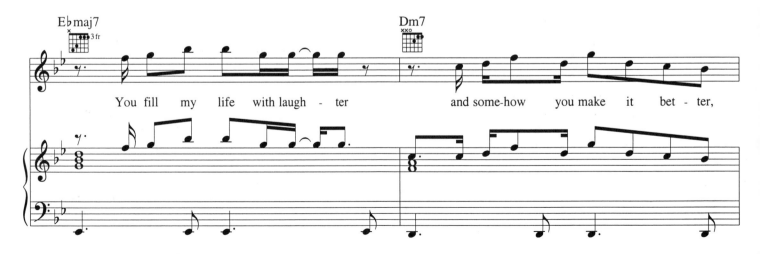

You fill my life with laugh - ter

and some-how you make it bet - ter,

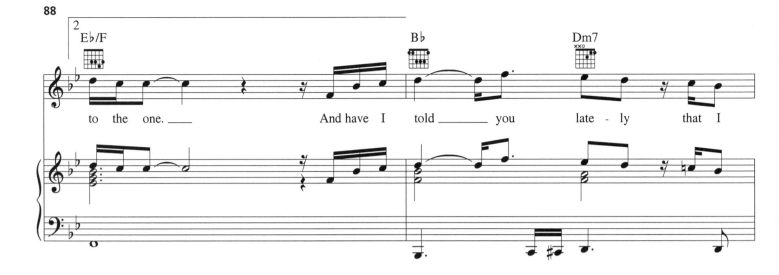

to the one. ___ And have I told _____ you late-ly that I

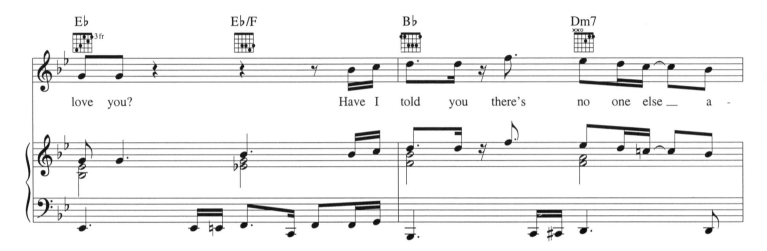

love you? Have I told you there's no one else ___ a-

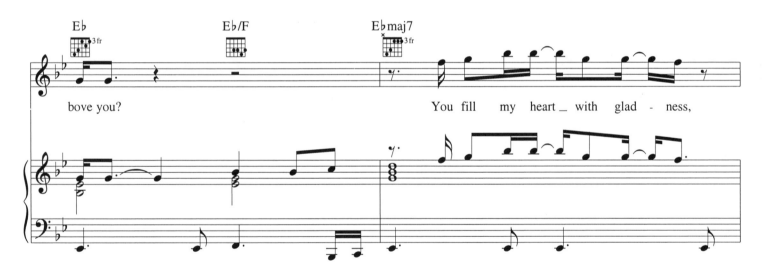

bove you? You fill my heart ___ with glad-ness,

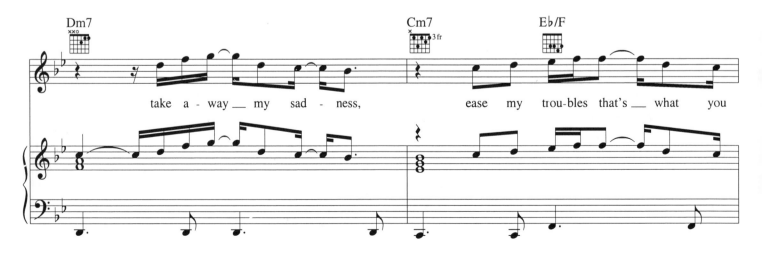

take a-way ___ my sad-ness, ease my trou-bles that's ___ what you

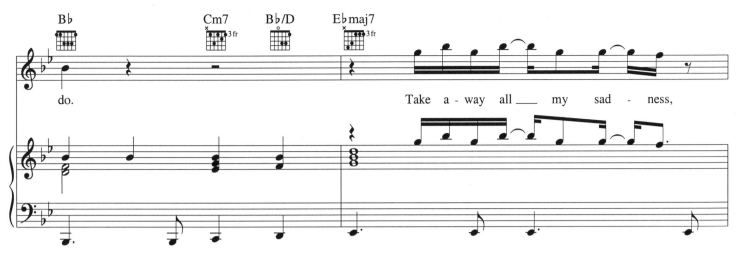

do.

Take a-way all ___ my sad-ness,

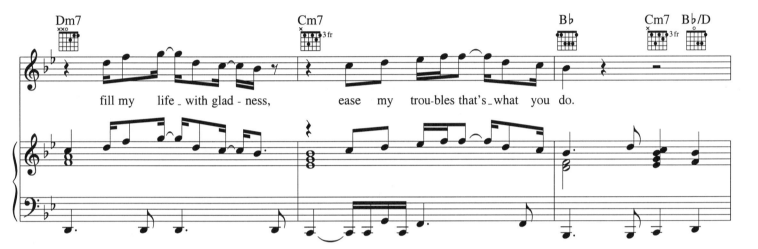

fill my life ___ with glad-ness, ease my trou-bles that's ___ what you do.

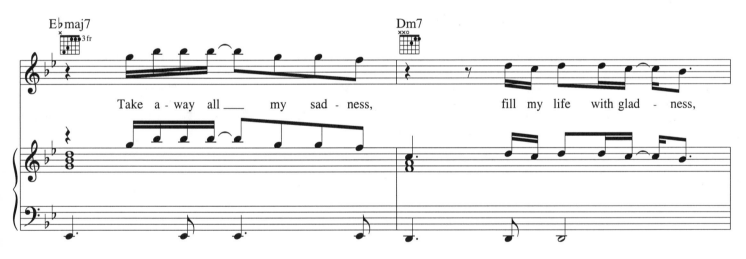

Take a-way all ___ my sad-ness, fill my life with glad - ness,

ease my trou-bles that's ___ what you do. _____

Hard To Say I'm Sorry

Words and Music by PETER CETERA
and DAVID FOSTER

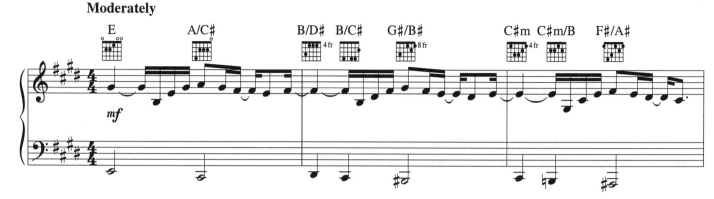

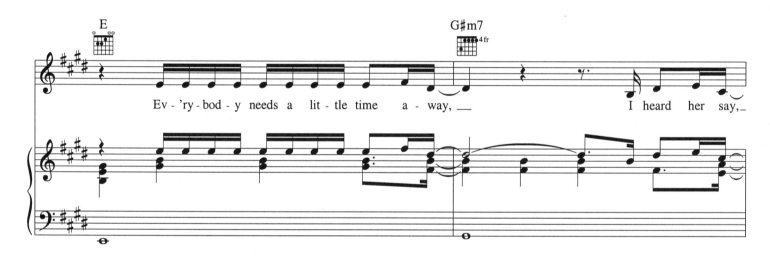

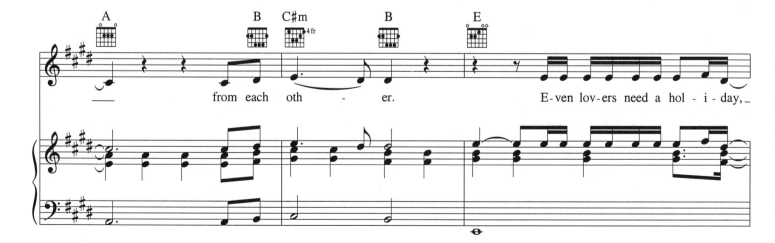

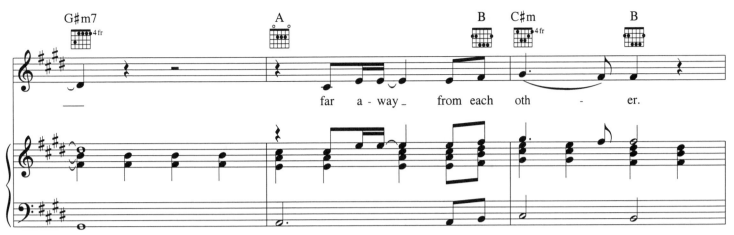

far a-way_ from each oth - er.

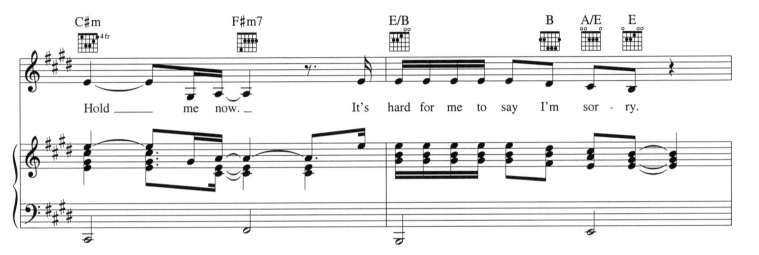

Hold _____ me now. _____ It's hard for me to say I'm sor - ry.

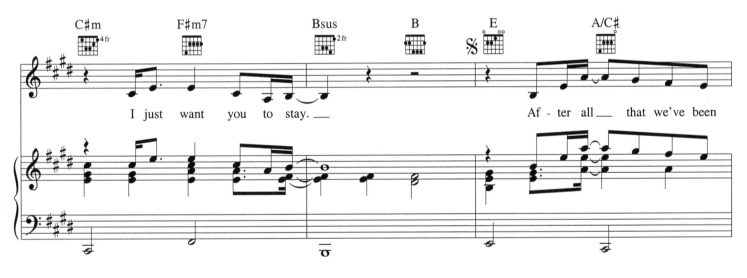

I just want you to stay. _____ Af - ter all_ that we've been

through, I will make it up_ to you. _____ I'll prom - ise to.

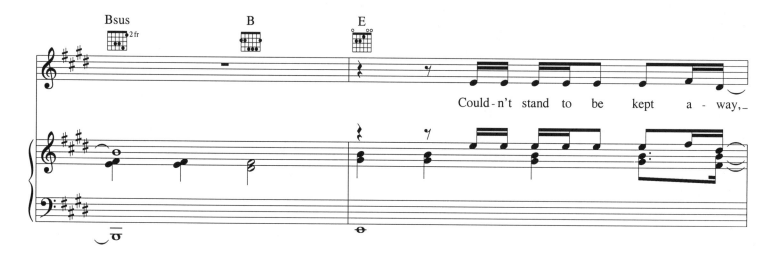

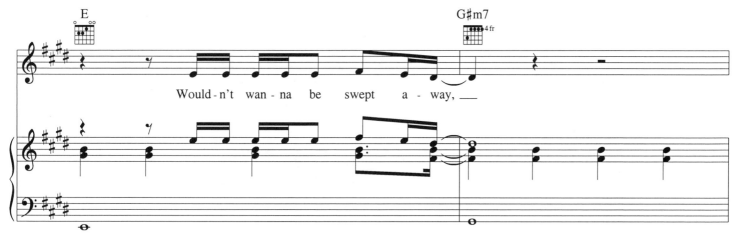

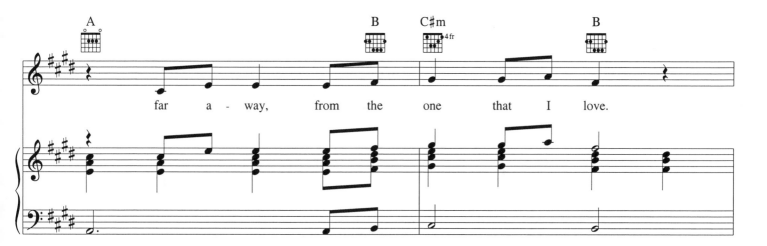

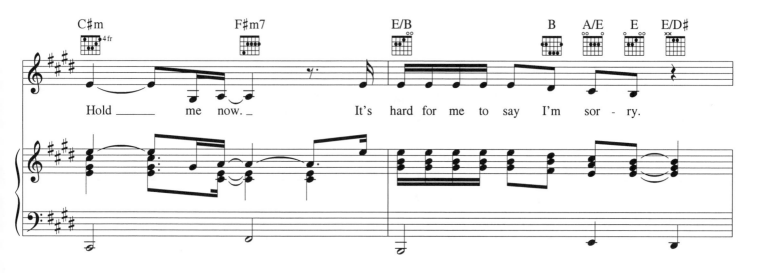

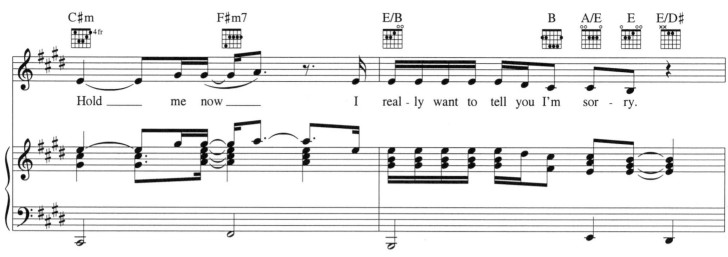

Hold ____ me now ____ I real-ly want to tell you I'm sor - ry.

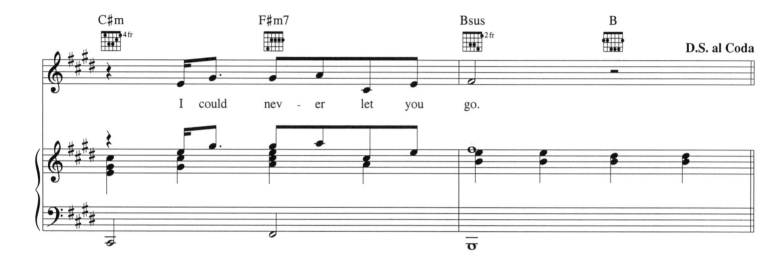

I could nev - er let you go.

D.S. al Coda

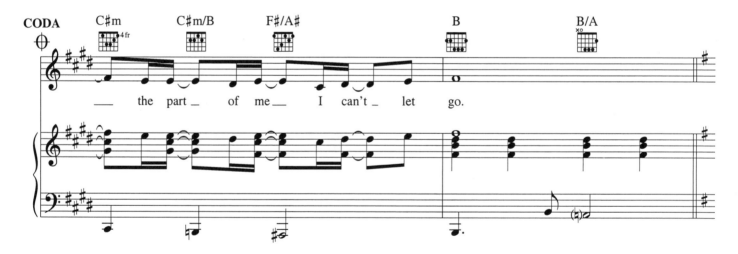

CODA

____ the part ____ of me ____ I can't ____ let go.

Af - ter all that we've_ been through, I will make it up ____

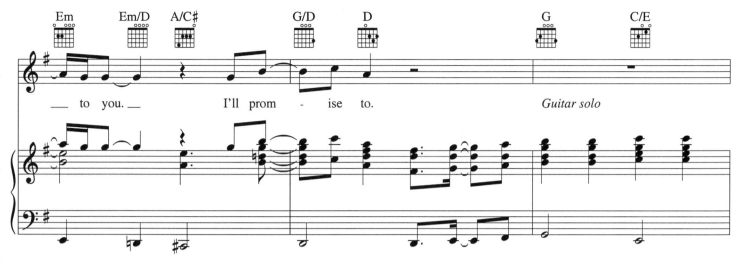

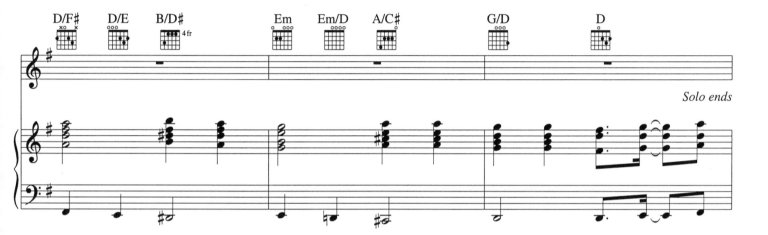

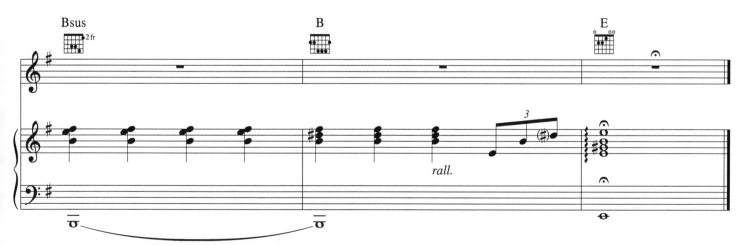

Here, There and Everywhere

Words and Music by JOHN LENNON
and PAUL McCARTNEY

Hero

Words and Music by MARIAH CAREY
and WALTER AFANASIEFF

and you'll fin - 'ly see __ the truth __ that a he - ro lies __ in you. __

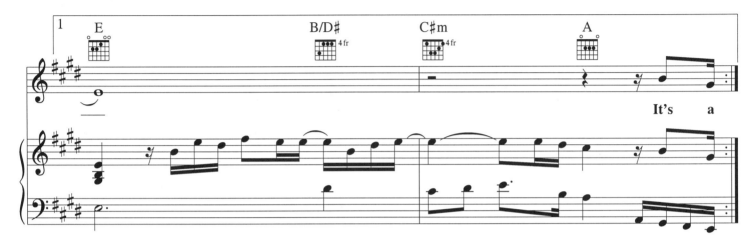

It's a

Lord knows __ dreams are hard_ to fol - low,

but don't let an - y - one __ tear them a - way. __ Hold __ on, __

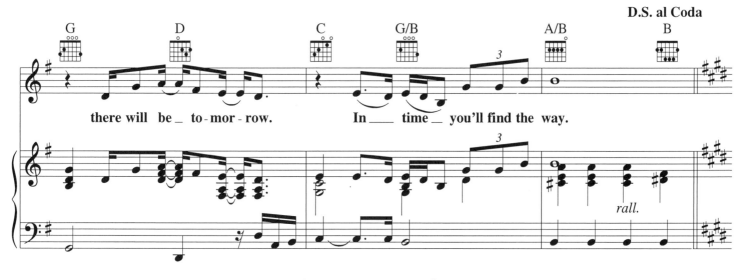

there will be _ to-mor-row. In ___ time _ you'll find the way.

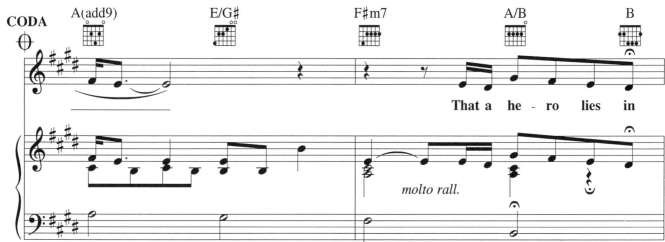

CODA

That a he - ro lies in

you, ___

that a he - ro lies in ___ you. ___

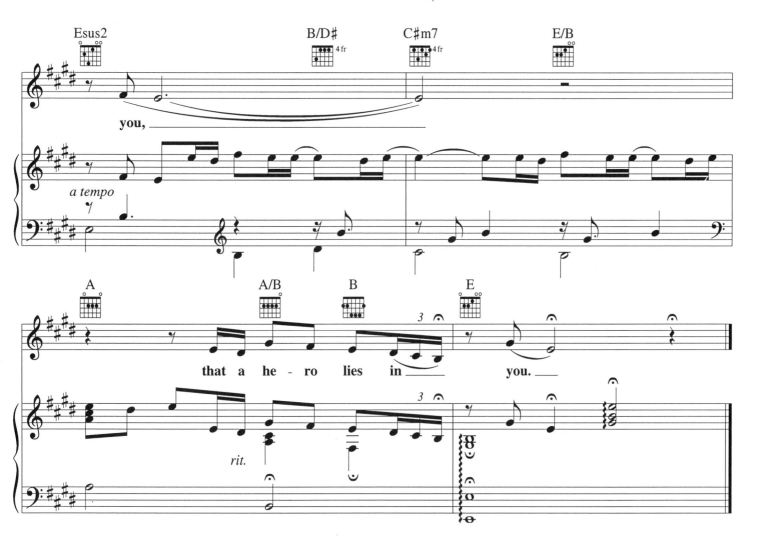

I Believe in You and Me

from the Touchstone Motion Picture THE PREACHER'S WIFE

Words and Music by DAVID WOLFERT
and SANDY LINZER

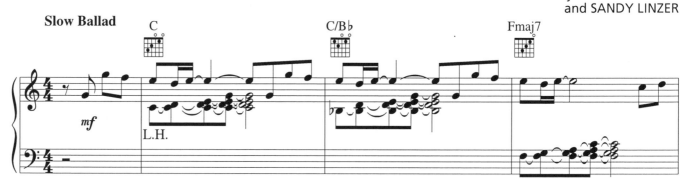

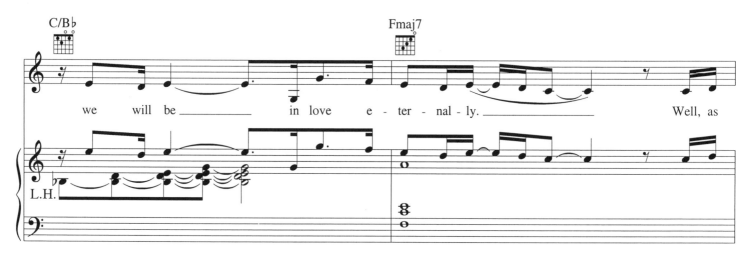

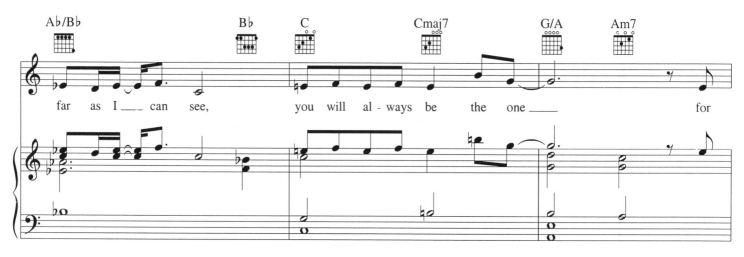

me, _____ oh, yes, you will. And I be-lieve in dreams _

___ a - gain. _____ I be-lieve that love will nev-er end. _____ And

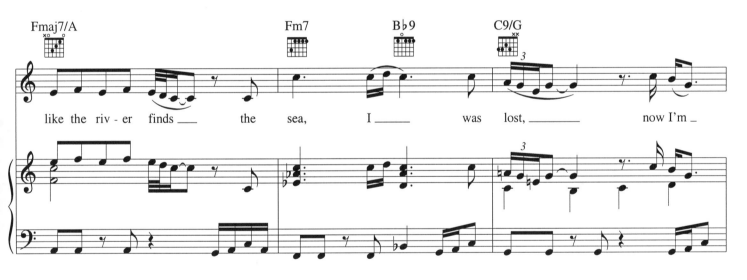

like the riv-er finds ___ the sea, I _____ was lost, _____ now I'm _

free _____ 'cause I be-lieve _ in you _ and me. I will nev-er leave _

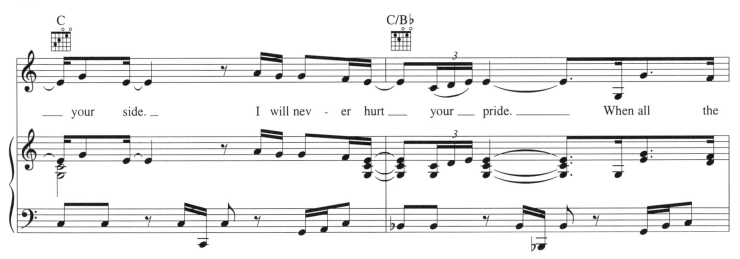

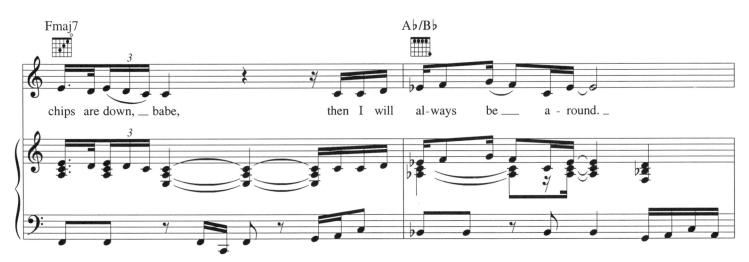

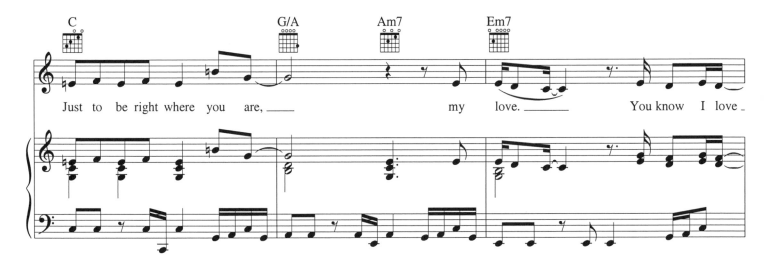

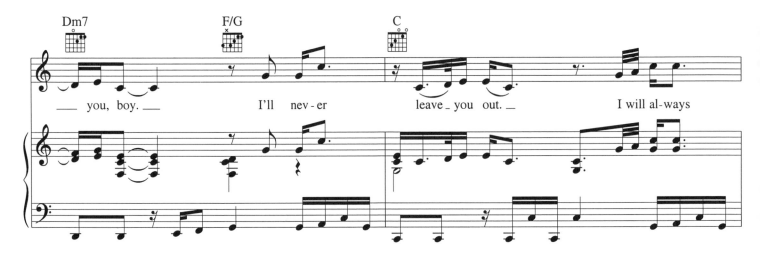

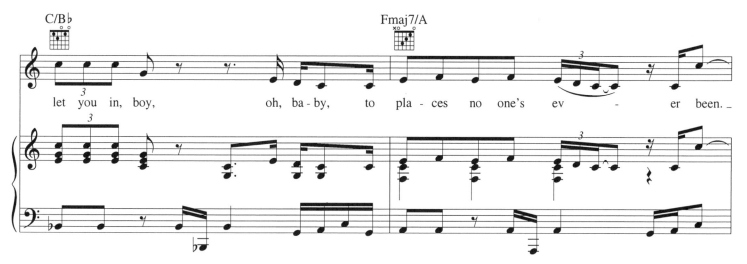

let you in, boy, oh, ba-by, to pla-ces no one's ev-er been.

Deep _____ in-side, _____ can't you see _____ that

I be-lieve _ in you _____ and me. May-be I'm a fool _____ to

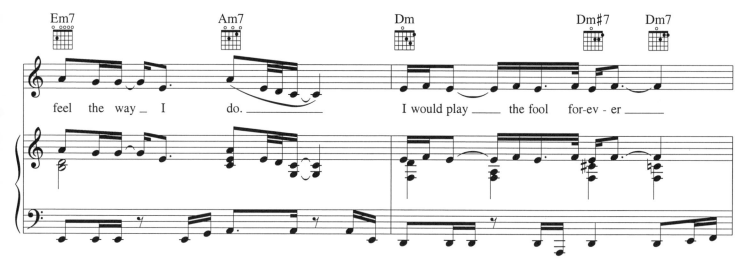

feel the way _ I do. _____ I would play ____ the fool for-ev-er ____

I be-lieve, _ I do be-lieve in you and me. See, I'm _

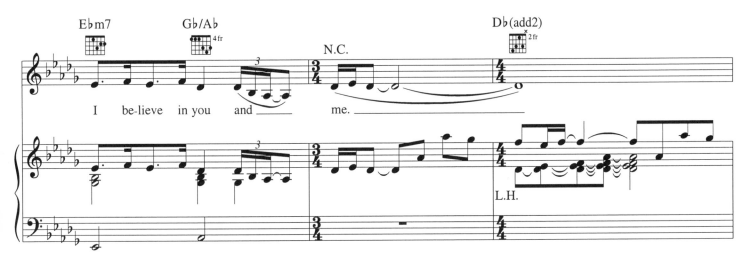

lost, _____ now I'm free _____ 'cause

I be-lieve in you and _____ me. _____

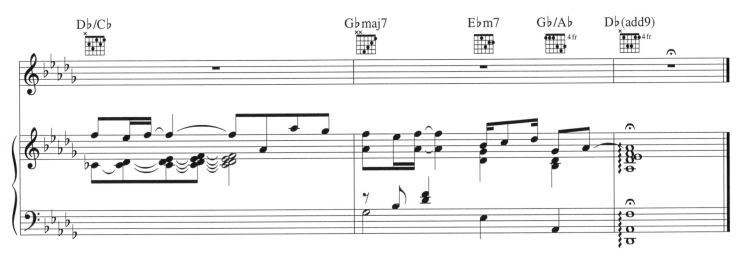

I Finally Found Someone

from THE MIRROR HAS TWO FACES

Words and Music by BARBRA STREISAND, MARVIN HAMLISCH,
R. J. LANGE and BRYAN ADAMS

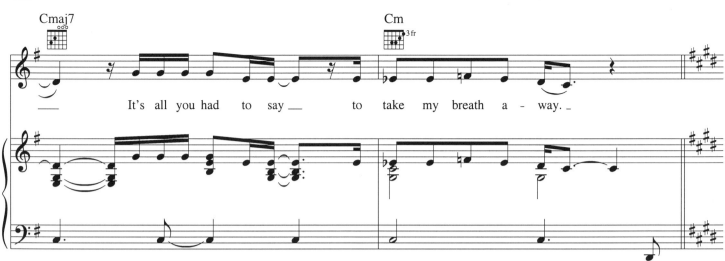

It's all you had to say ___ to take my breath a - way. ___

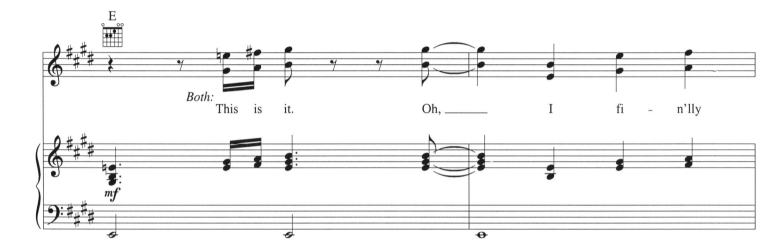

Both: This is it. Oh, ___ I fi - n'lly

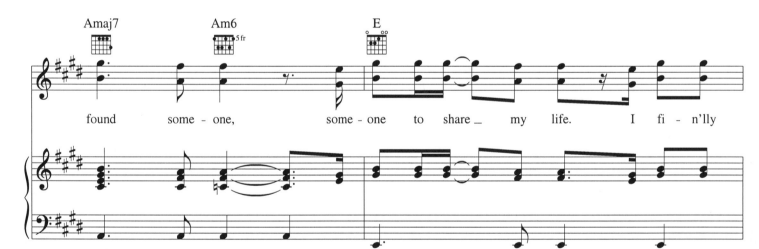

found some - one, some - one to share ___ my life. I fi - n'lly

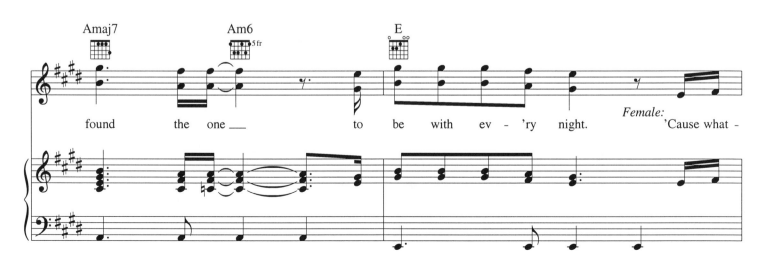

found the one ___ to be with ev - 'ry night. *Female:* 'Cause what -

ev - er I do, _____ *Male:* it's just got to be you. *Both:* My

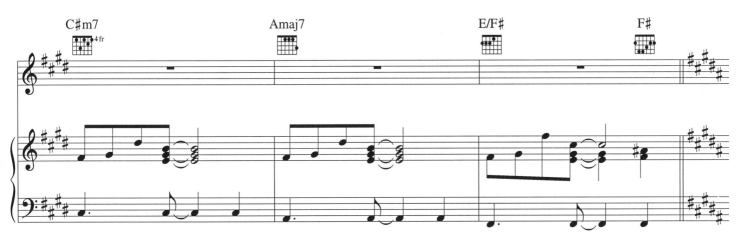

life has just be-gun. I fi - n'lly found some - one. _____

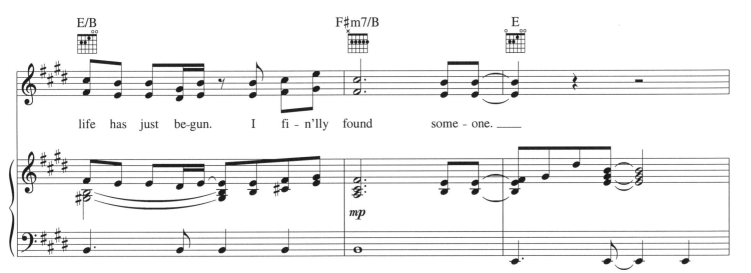

Male: Did I keep you wait - ing? I a - pol - o - gize. _____
Female: I did - n't mind. _____ Ba - by, that's fine. _____

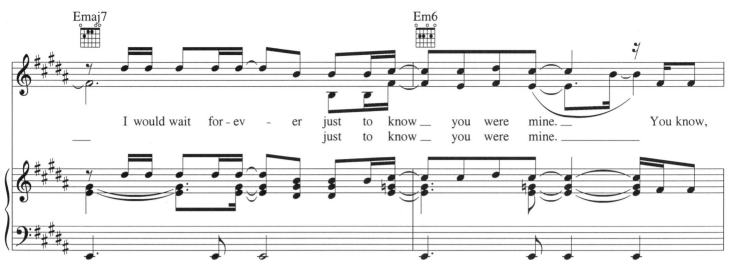

I would wait for- ev - er just to know __ you were mine. __ You know,
__ just to know __ you were mine. __

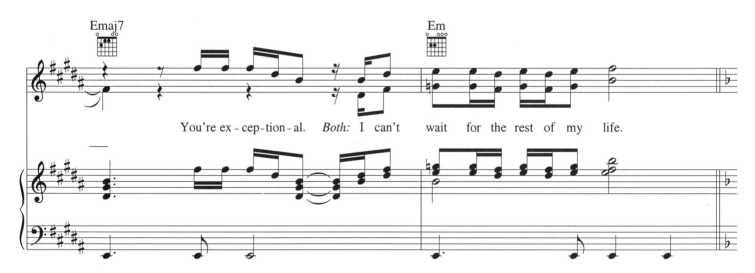

I love your hair. __ I love what you wear.
Are you sure it looks right? __ Is - n't it too tight? __

You're ex - cep-tion- al. *Both:* I can't wait for the rest of my life.

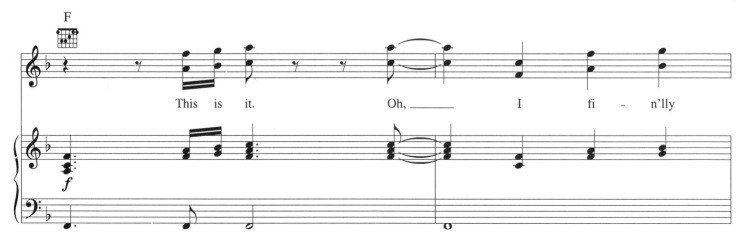

This is it. Oh, __ I fi - n'lly

found some-one, some-one to share __ my life. I fi-n'lly

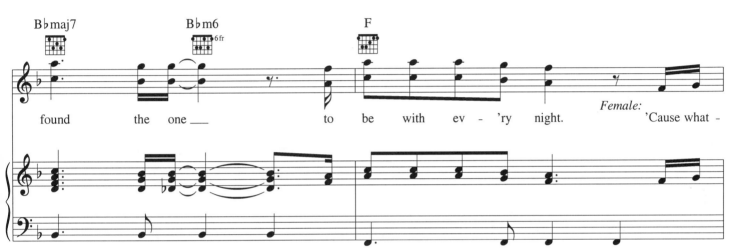

found the one __ to be with ev-'ry night.

Female: 'Cause what-

ev-er I do, __

Male: it's just got to be you.

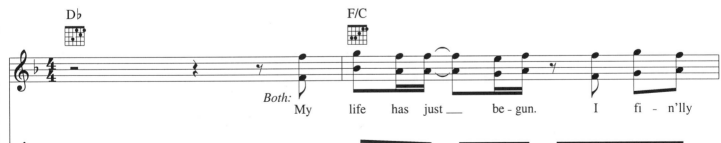

Both: My life has just __ be-gun. I fi-n'lly

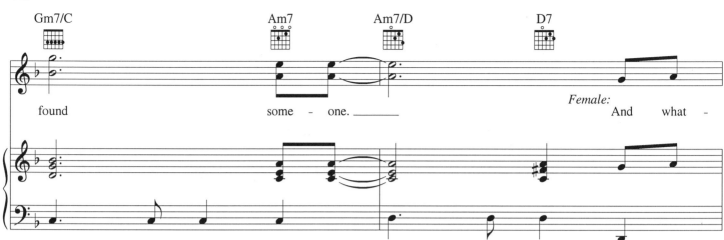

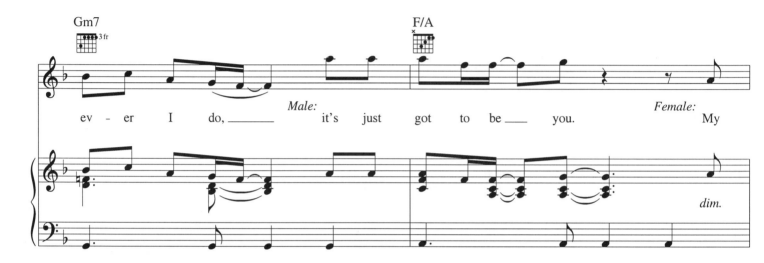

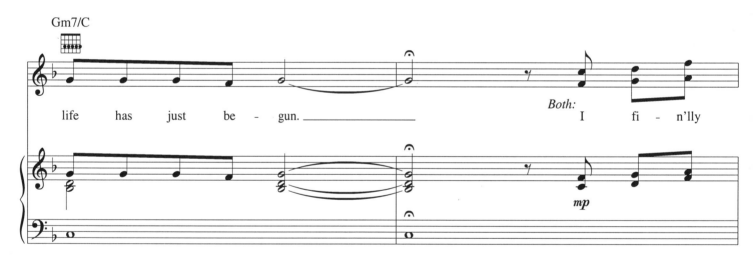

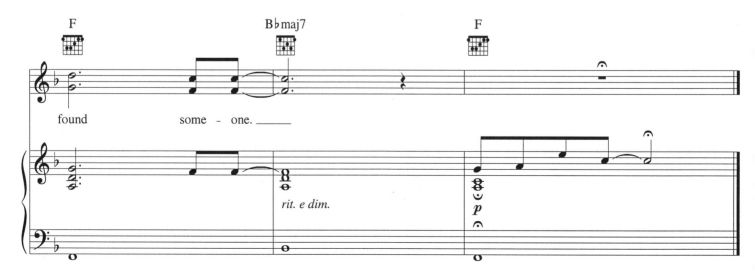

I Will Remember You

Theme from THE BROTHERS McMULLEN

Words and Music by SARAH McLACHLAN,
SEAMUS EGAN and DAVE MERENDA

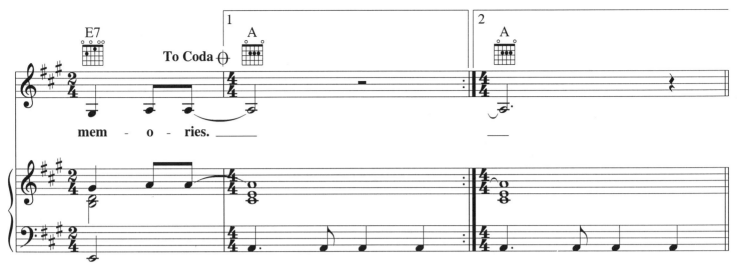

mem - o - ries.

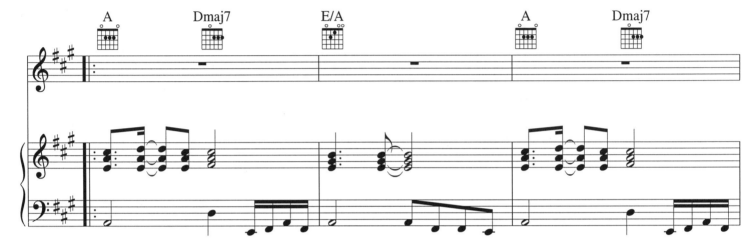

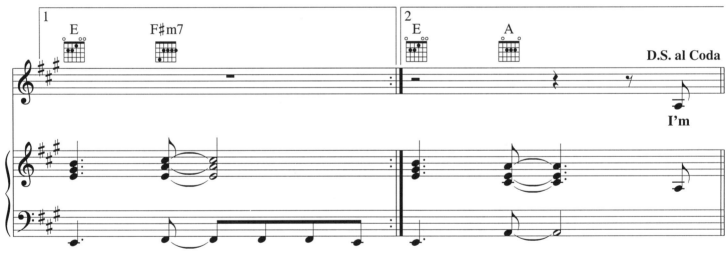

D.S. al Coda

I'm

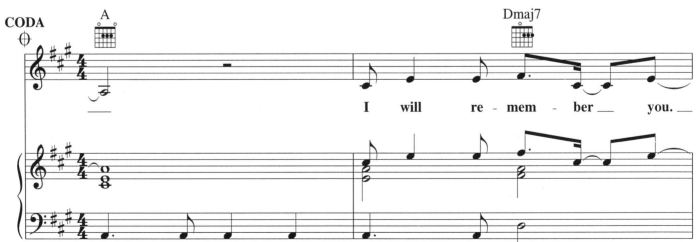

CODA

I will re - mem - ber you.

I Write the Songs

Words and Music by
BRUCE JOHNSTON

I've been a-live for-ev-er,
My home lies deep with-in you

and I wrote the ver-y first song. ___
and I've got my own place in your soul.

I put the words and the
Now, when I look out

mel-o-dies to-geth-er, I am mu-sic, and I write the songs. ___
through your eyes ___ I'm young a-gain, e-ven though I'm ver-y old. ___

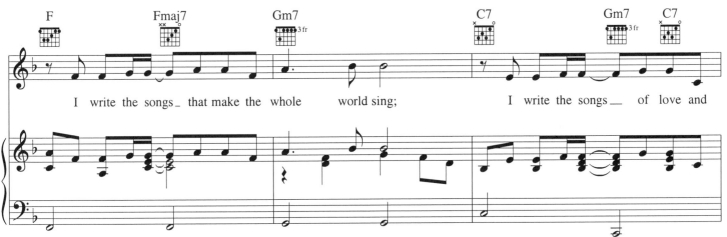

I write the songs_ that make the whole world sing; I write the songs_ of love and

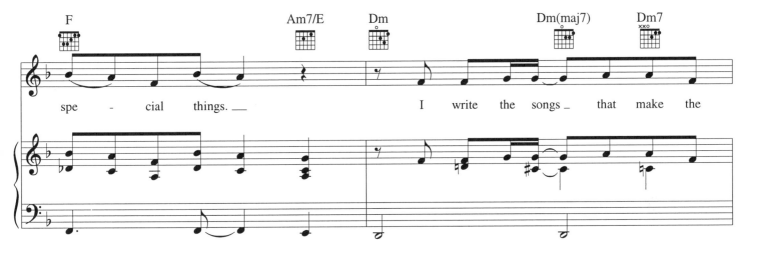

spe - cial things. __ I write the songs_ that make the

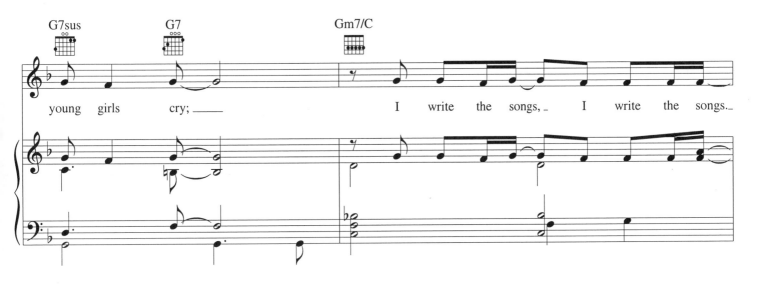

young girls cry; ___ I write the songs, _ I write the songs._

Imagine

Words and Music by
JOHN LENNON

It is-n't hard____ to do.____
I won-der if you____ can.____

Noth-ing to kill____ or die____
No need for greed____ or hun -

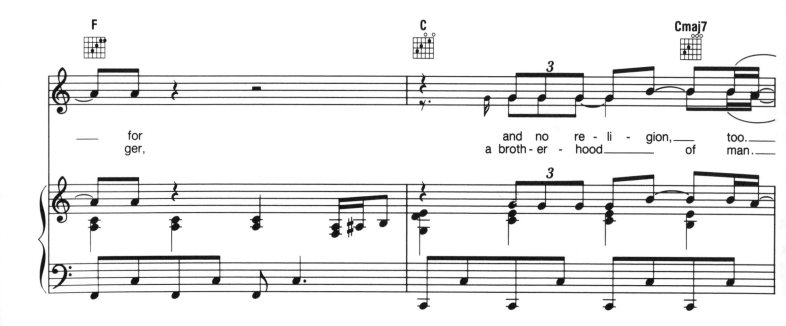

____ for
ger,

and no re-li - gion,____ too.____
a broth-er - hood____ of man.____

In My Life

Words and Music by JOHN LENNON
and PAUL McCARTNEY

Moderately

There are plac- es I'll re- mem- ber all my
But of all these friends and lov- ers there is

life,_____ though some have changed.__ Some for- ev- er, not for
no_____ one com- pares with you.__ And these mem - 'ries lose for their

bet- ter; Some have gone_____ and some re- main.__ All these
mean- ing when I think of_ love as some- thing new.__ Tho' I

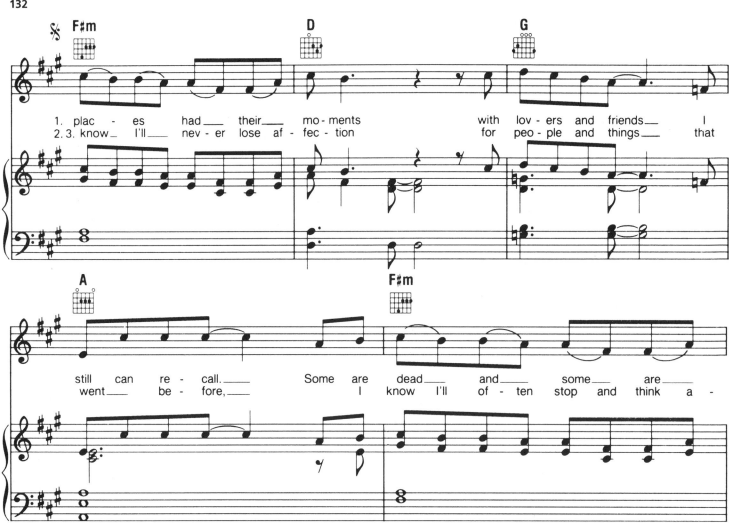

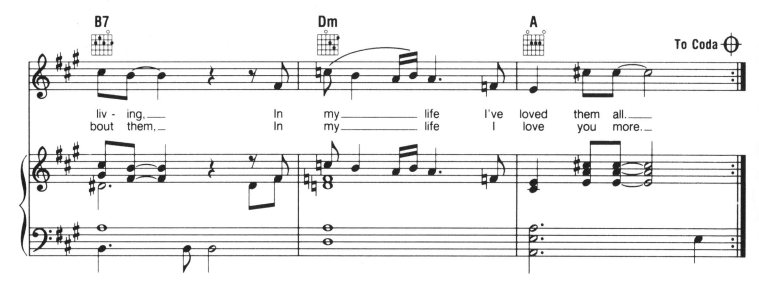

It's All Coming Back to Me Now

Words and Music by
JIM STEINMAN

com-ing back __ to me. It's so hard to re - sist, __ and it's all __
com-ing back __ to me. The flesh and the fan - ta - sies all __

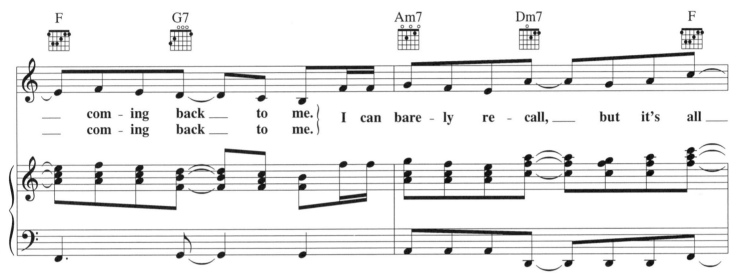

com-ing back __ to me. I can bare-ly re-call, __ but it's all __
com-ing back __ to me.

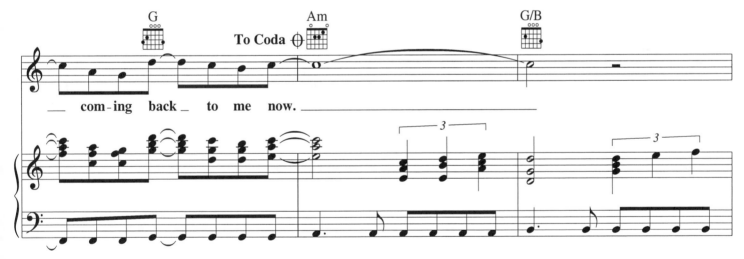

com-ing back __ to me now. _____

D.S. al Coda

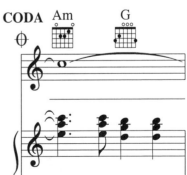

CODA

Just My Imagination
(Running Away with Me)

Words and Music by NORMAN J. WHITFIELD
and BARRETT STRONG

Each day through my win-dow I
Soon we'll be

watch her as she pass-es by. _____ I
mar-ried and raise a fam-i-ly. A

say to my-self, "You're such __ a luck-y guy. _____
coz-y lit-tle home out in the coun-try with two chil-dren, may-be three.

To have a girl like her _____ is tru-ly
I tell you, I _____ can vis-ual-

a dream come _ true. _____ Out of all the fel-lows in the
ize it ____ all. _____ This could-n't be a dream, far too

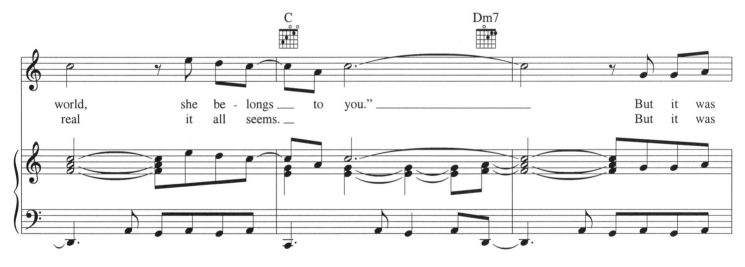

world, she be-longs ___ to you." _____ But it was
real it all seems. _ But it was

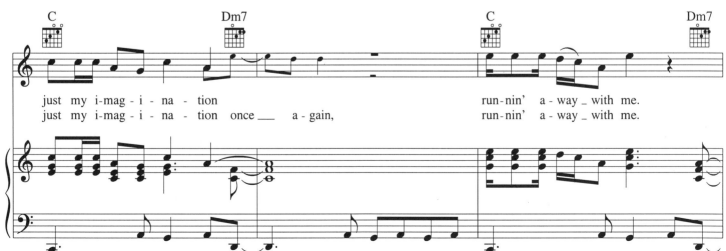

just my i-mag-i-na-tion runnin' a-way _ with me.
just my i-mag-i-na-tion once ___ a-gain, runnin' a-way _ with me.

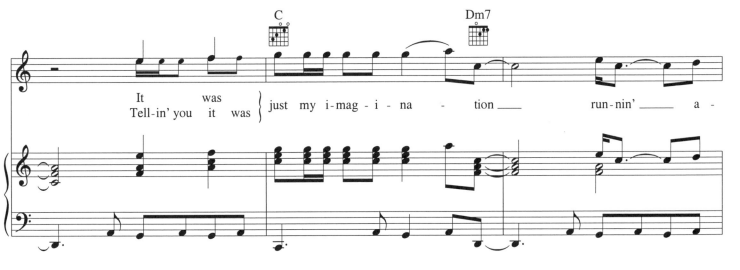

It was { Tell-in' you it was } just my i-mag-i-na - tion _____ run-nin' _____ a-

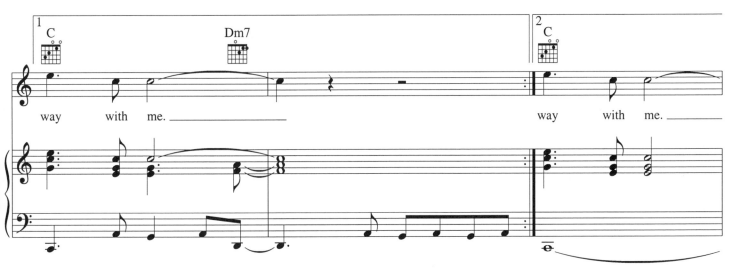

way with me. _____ way with me. _____

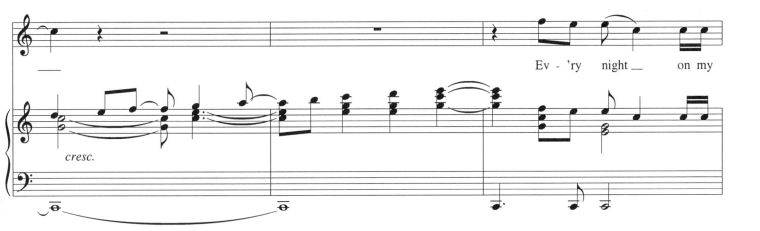

_____ Ev - 'ry night _ on my

knees I pray, _____ ("Dear Lord,) _ hear my plea. ____

Don't ev-er let an-oth-er take her love from me, or I would

sure-ly die." _____ Her love is heav-en-ly.

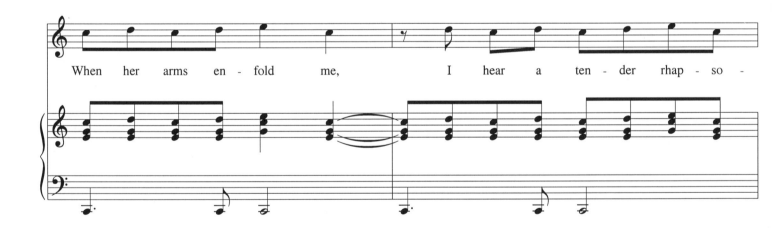

When her arms en-fold me, I hear a ten-der rhap-so-

dy. But in re-al-i-ty, she does-n't e-ven know me.

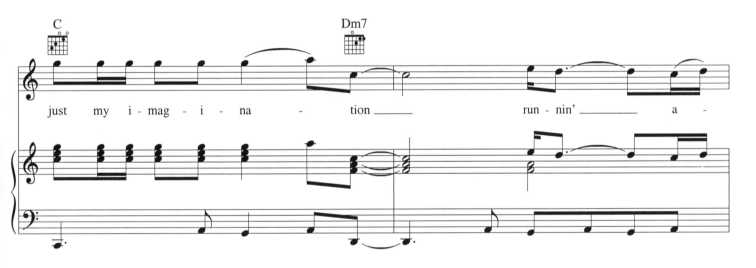

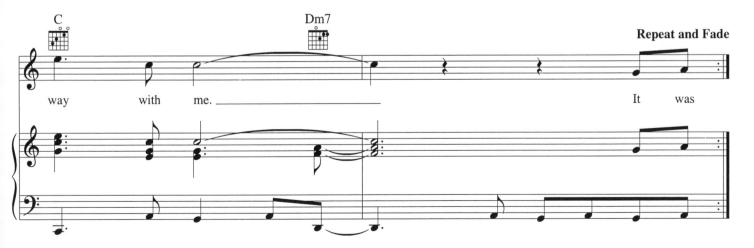

The Keeper of the Stars

Words and Music by KAREN STALEY,
DANNY MAYO and DICKEY LEE

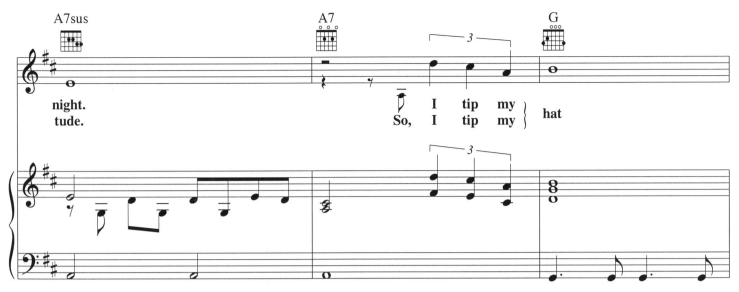

night.
tude.
So, I tip my hat

to the Keep - er of ___ the Stars.

He sure knew what he ___ was do - in' ___

when he joined these two hearts.
I hold ev - 'ry -

thing ... when I hold __ you in my

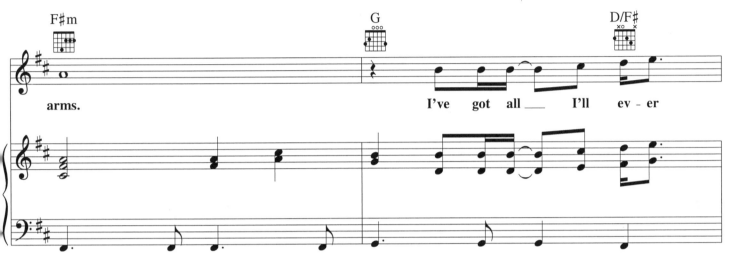

arms. ... I've got all __ I'll ev - er

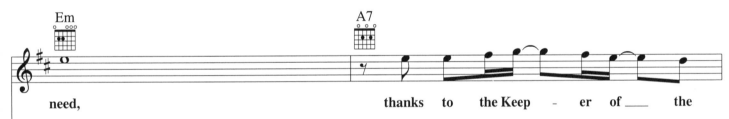

need, ... thanks to the Keep - er of __ the

Stars. _____ Stars. _____

It was_ no ac - ci - dent,_

me find - ing you.

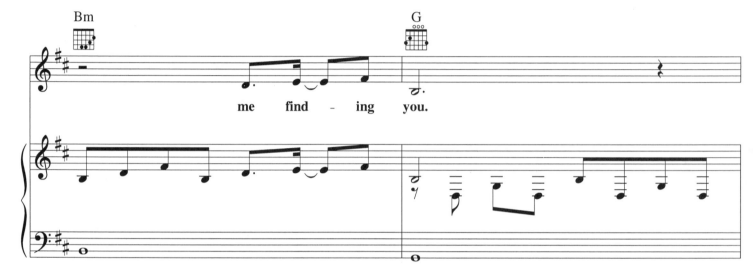

Some - one had a hand in it ____

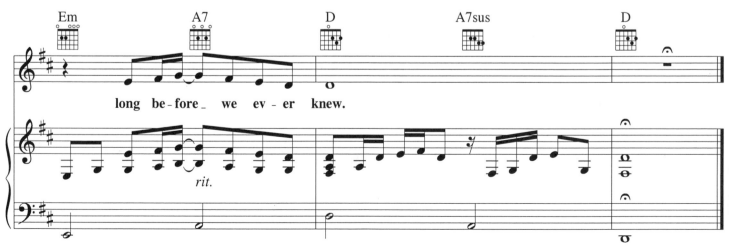

long be - fore_ we ev - er knew.

rit.

Killing Me Softly With His Song

Words by NORMAN GIMBEL
Music by CHARLES FOX

killing me soft - ly with his _____ song, kill-ing me soft - ly_____ with his_

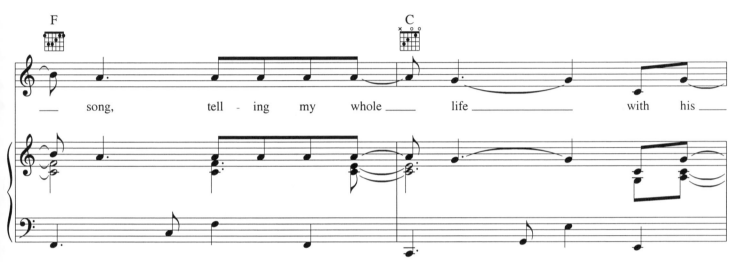

_____ song, tell - ing my whole _____ life _____ with his _____

_____ words, kill - ing me soft - ly _____ with his song._

Let It Be

Words and Music by JOHN LENNON
and PAUL McCARTNEY

Longer

Words and Music by
DAN FOGELBERG

Moderate Ballad

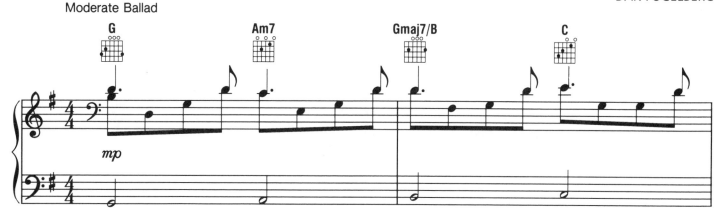

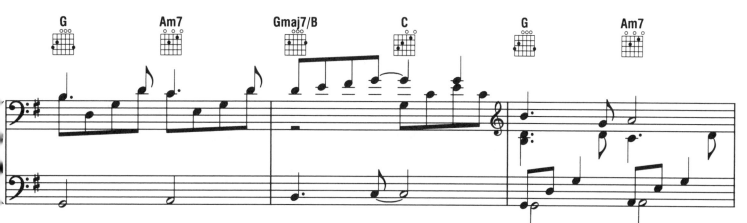

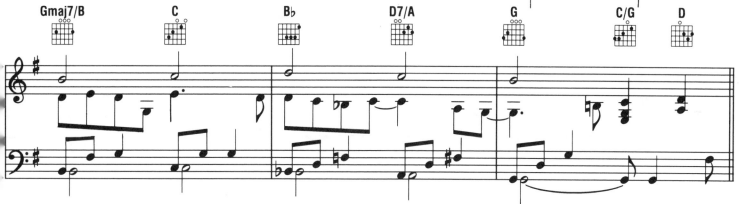

Long - er than_ there've been fish - es in the o - cean,
Strong - er than_ an - y moun - tain cath - e - dral.
Through the years_ as the fi - re starts to mel - low,

high - er than___ an - y bird ev - er flew,___
tru - er than___ an - y tree ev - er grew,___
burn - ing lines___ in the book of our lives.___

Though the

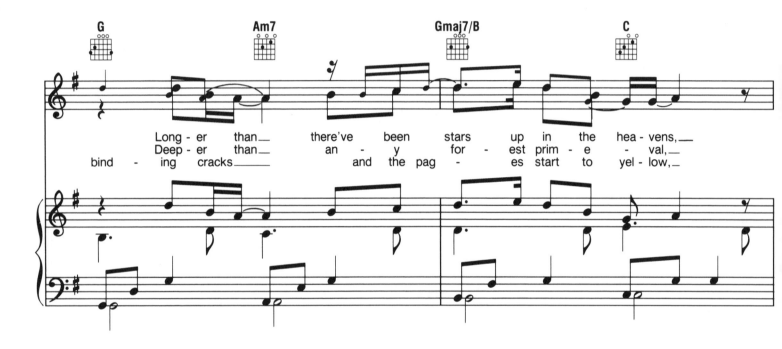

Long - er than___ there've been stars up in the hea - vens,___
Deep - er than___ an - y for - est prim - e - val,___
bind - ing cracks___ and the pag - es start to yel - low,___

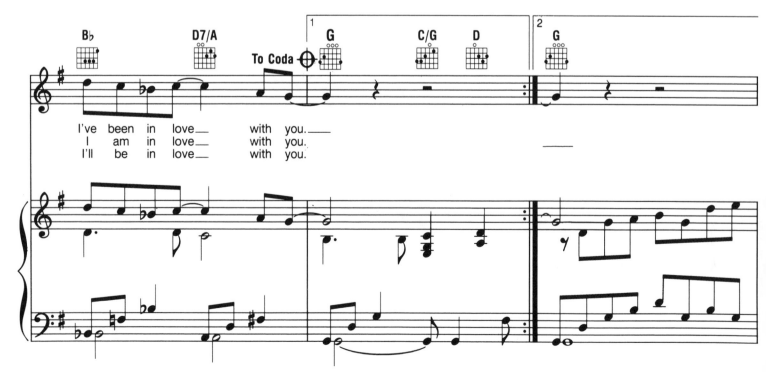

I've been in love___ with you.___
I am in love___ with you.___
I'll be in love___ with you.

Memory
from CATS

Music by ANDREW LLOYD WEBBER
Text by TREVOR NUNN after T.S. ELIOT

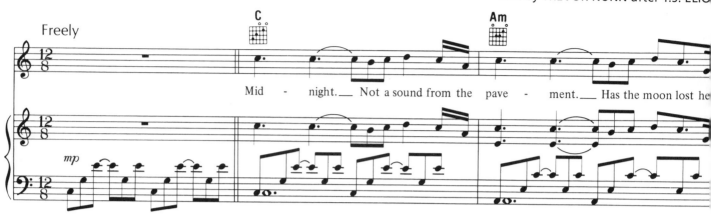

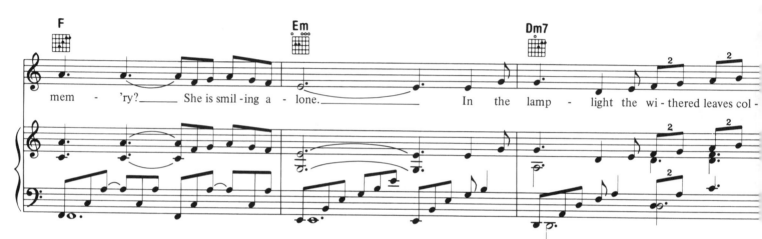

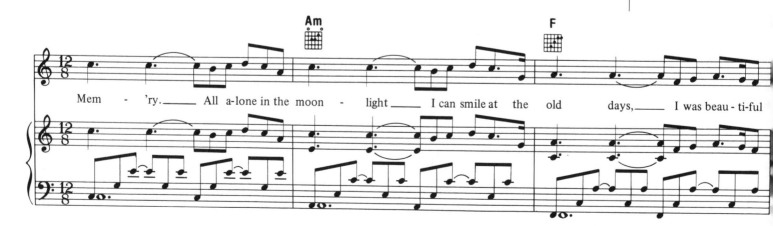

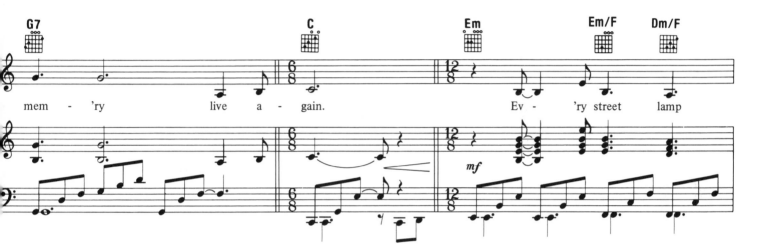

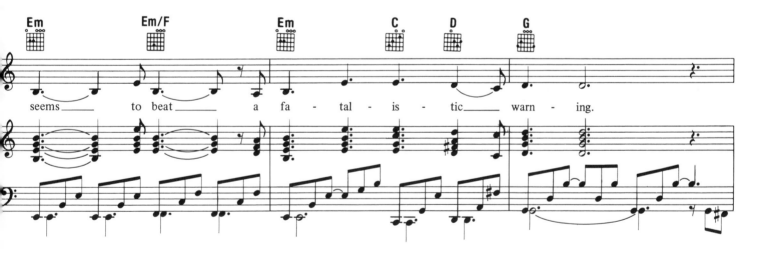

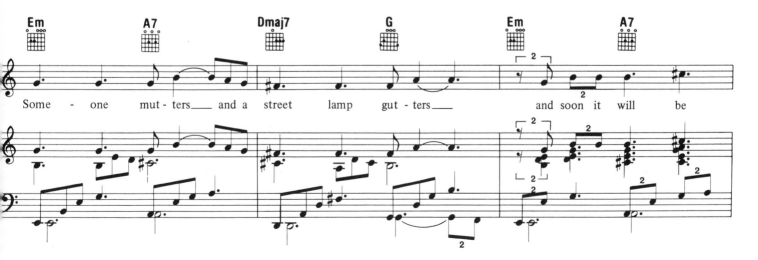

Michelle

Words and Music by JOHN LENNON
and PAUL McCARTNEY

love you, I love you, I love you,
need you, I need you, I need you.
want you, I want you, I need you.

That's all I want to say.
I need to make you see
I think you know by now.

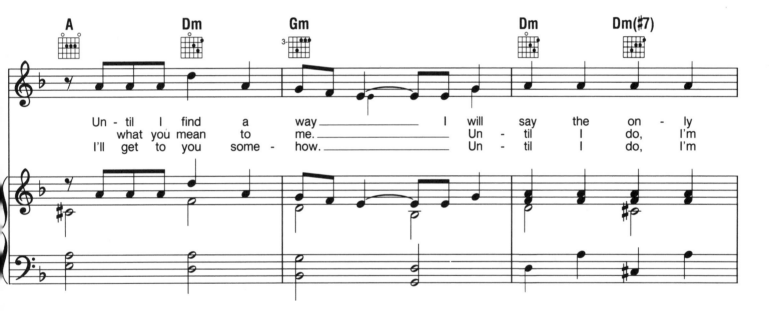

Un - til I find a way ___ I will say the on - ly
what you mean to me. ___ Un - til I do, I'm
I'll get to you some - how. ___ Un - til I do, I'm

words I know that you'll un - der - stand.
hop - ing you that will know what I mean. I
tell - ing you, so you'll un - der -

Mona Lisa

from the Paramount Picture CAPTAIN CAREY, U.S.A.

Words and Music by JAY LIVINGSTON
and RAY EVANS

Moon River
from the Paramount Picture BREAKFAST AT TIFFANY'S

Words by JOHNNY MERCER
Music by HENRY MANCINI

My Cherie Amour

Words and Music by STEVIE WONDER,
SYLVIA MOY and HENRY COSBY

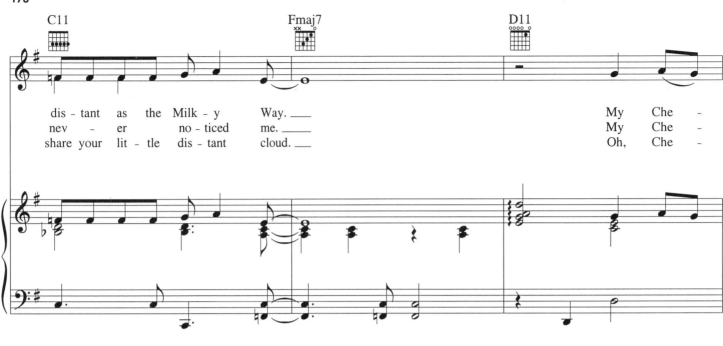

dis - tant as the Milk - y Way. ___ My Che -
nev - er no - ticed me. ___ My Che -
share your lit - tle dis - tant cloud. ___ Oh, Che -

rie A - mour, ___ pret - ty lit - tle one that I _____ a - dore, ___
rie A - mour, ___ won't you tell me how could you _____ ig - nore ___
rie A - mour, ___ pret - ty lit - tle one that I _____ a - dore, ___

To Coda ⊕

you're the on - ly girl my heart ___ beats for; ___ how I wish that you were mine.
that be - hind that lit - tle smile ___ I wore, ___ how I wish that you were mine. ___
you're the on - ly girl my heart ___ beats for; ___ how I wish that you were mine. ___

My Heart Will Go On
(Love Theme from 'Titanic')
from the Paramount and Twentieth Century Fox Motion Picture TITANIC

Music by JAMES HORNER
Lyric by WILL JENNINGS

Ev - 'ry night in my dreams I see you, I feel you, that is how I know you go on.

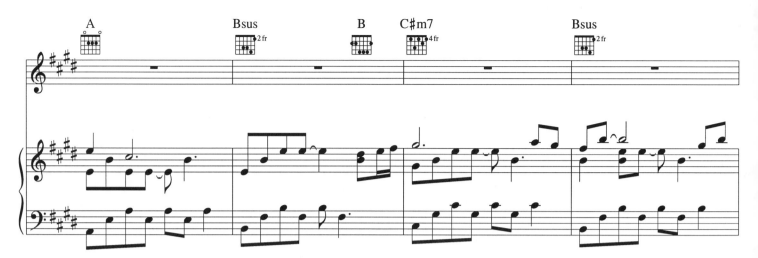

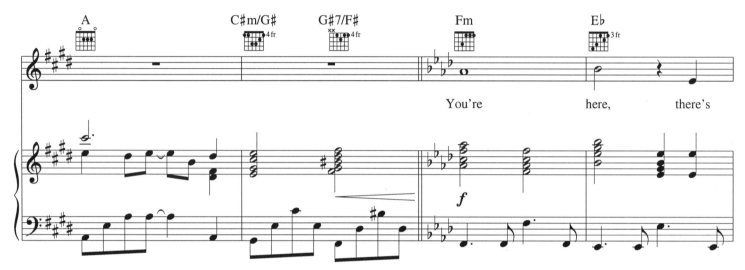

You're here, there's

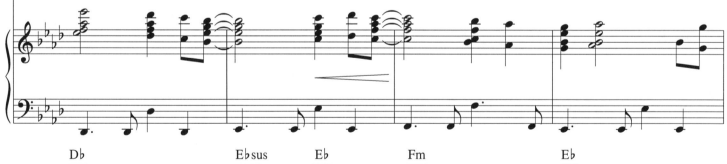

noth - ing I fear ___ and I know ___ that my heart will go

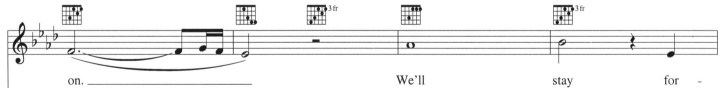

on. _____ We'll stay for -

Raindrops Keep Fallin' on My Head

Lyric by HAL DAVID
Music by BURT BACHARACH

Rhythmically

Rain - drops keep fall - in' on my head, and just like the guy whose feet are too big for his bed, noth - in' seems to fit. Those rain - drops are fall - in' on my head. They keep fall - in' so I just did me some talk - in' to the

Sometimes When We Touch

Words by DAN HILL
Music by BARRY MANN

see the real_____ you.
trapped with-in_____ my youth.
pas - sion flares_____ a - gain.

And

some-times when we touch,___ the hon-es-ty's too— much.___

And I

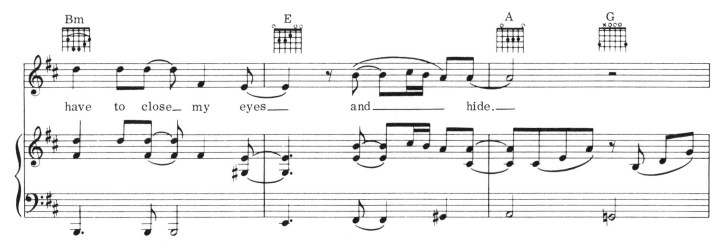

have to close___ my eyes___ and_____ hide.___

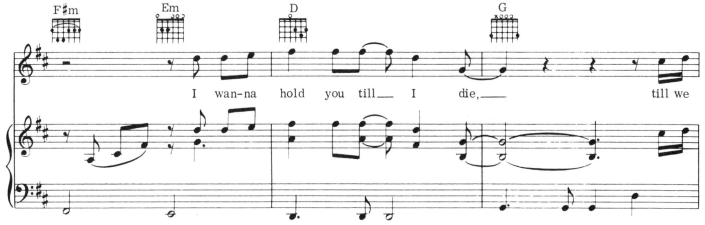

I wan-na hold you till___ I die,___

till we

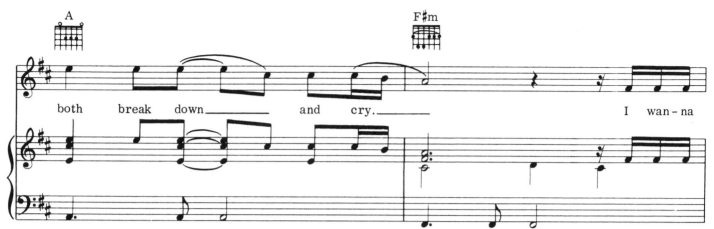

both break down _____ and cry._____ I wan-na

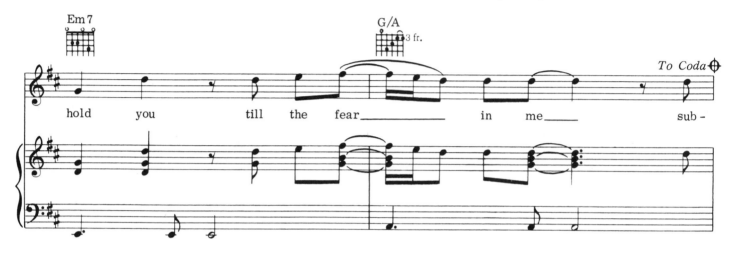

hold you till the fear_____ in me_____ sub-

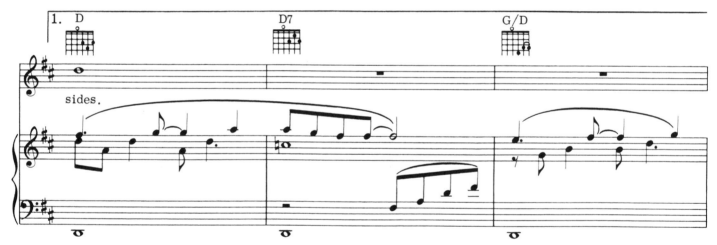

sides.

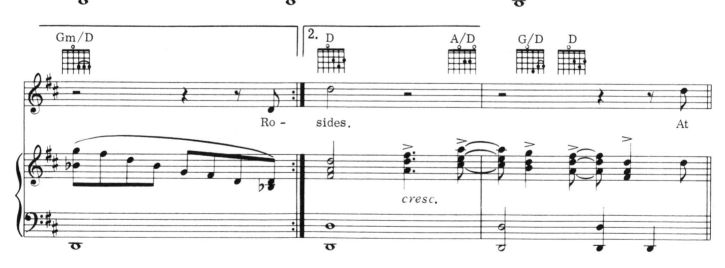

Ro - sides. At

Ribbon in the Sky

Words and Music by
STEVIE WONDER

Slowly, with expression

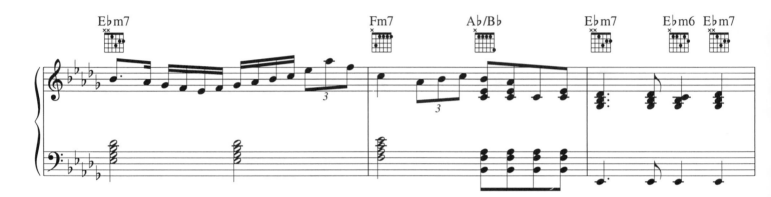

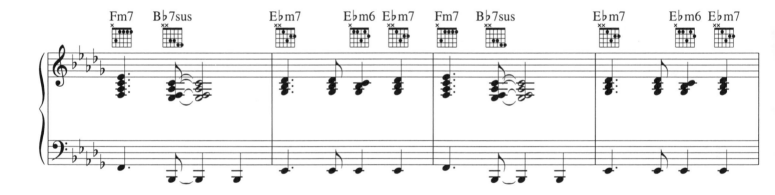

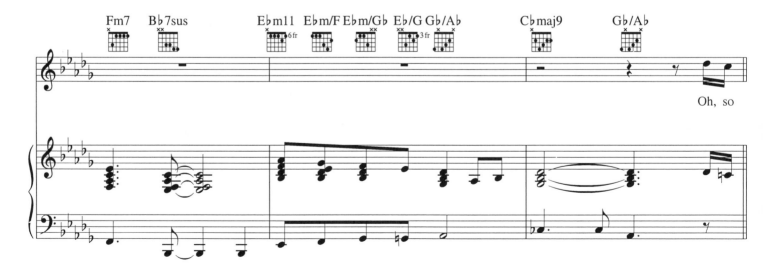

Oh, so

luck - y chance, ___ but what is _____ that was al - ways meant ___ is our

rib - bon in the sky for our love; ___ love ___ we can't lose, ___

_____ with God on our side. ___ We'll find strength _____ in each

tear we cry. ___ From now on _____ it will be you and I ____ and our

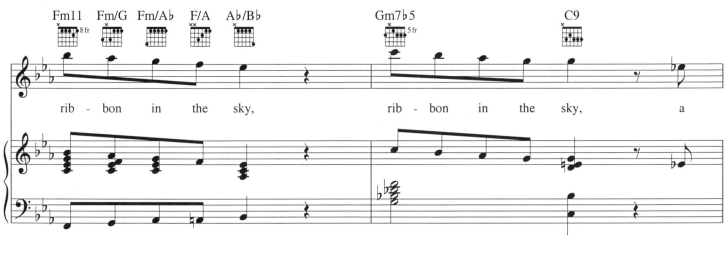

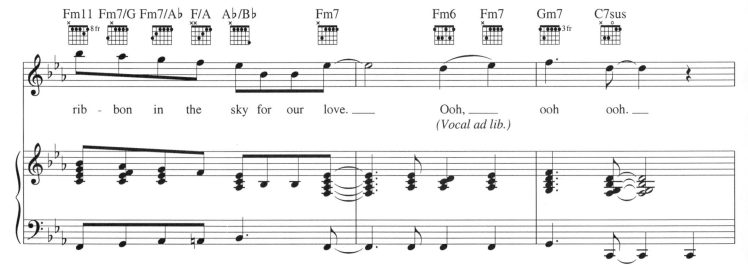

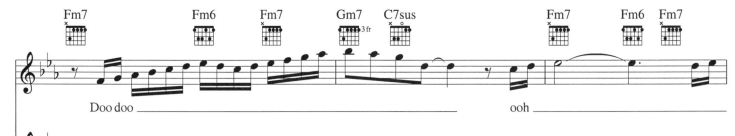

Save the Best for Last

Words and Music by PHIL GALDSTON,
JON LIND and WENDY WALDMAN

Some - times the snow ____ comes down ____ in June.
____ you came ____ to me ____
____ comes down ____ in June.

____ Some - times the sun ____ goes 'round ____ the moon. ____
when some sil - ly girl ____ had set ____ you free. ____
Some - times the sun ____ goes 'round ____ the moon. ____

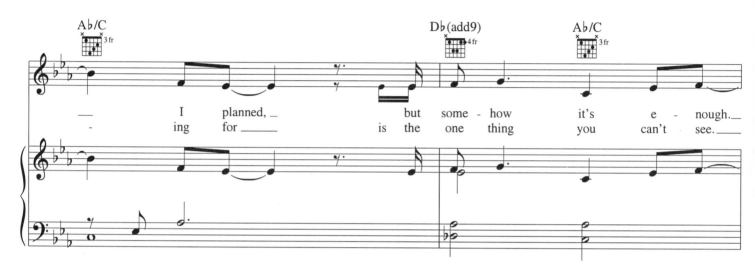

Just when I thought _____ our chance_ had passed,_

_ you go and save _____ the best ___ for last. ___

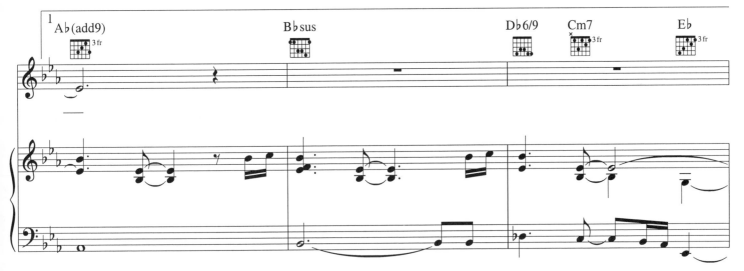

All of the nights_ ___

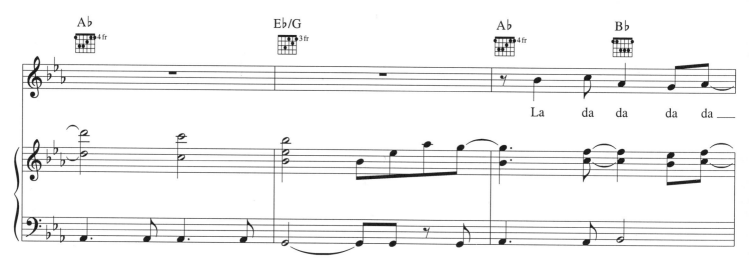

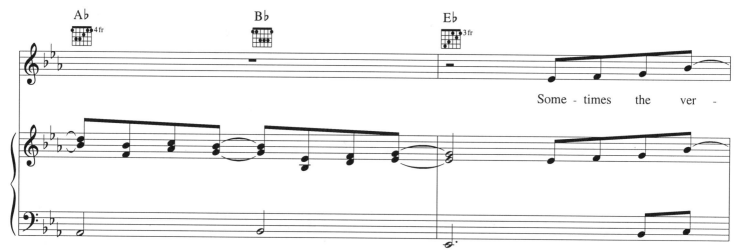

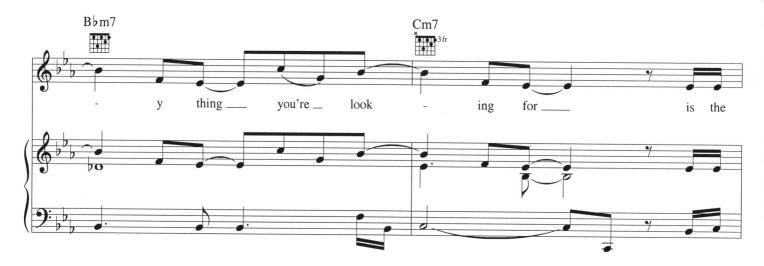

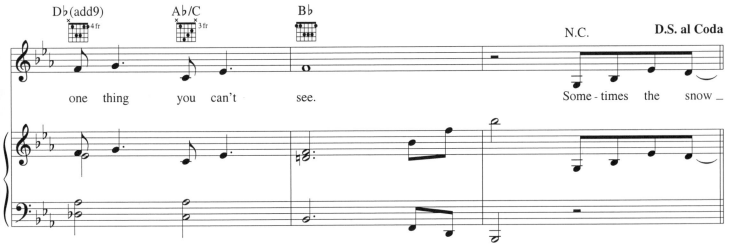

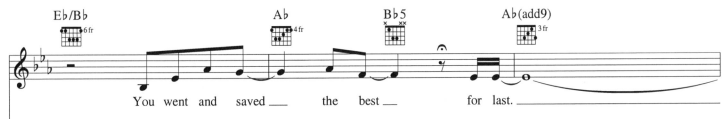

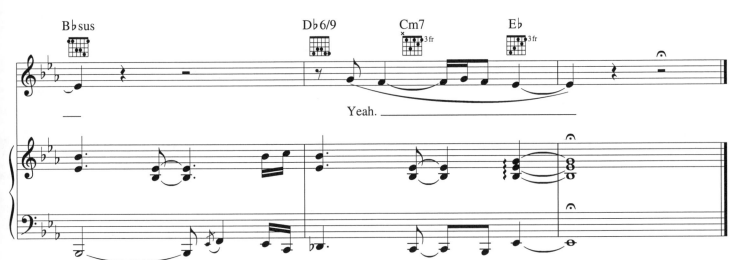

Something

Words and Music by
GEORGE HARRISON

Somewhere Out There
from AN AMERICAN TAIL

Words and Music by JAMES HORNER,
BARRY MANN and CYNTHIA WEIL

Moderately, with expression

Some - where ___ out there be - neath the pale moon - light ___ some - one's think - in' of me and

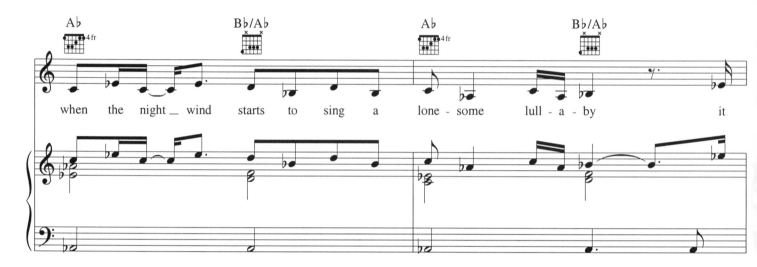

helps to think _ we might _ be wish - in' on the same _ bright _ star. And

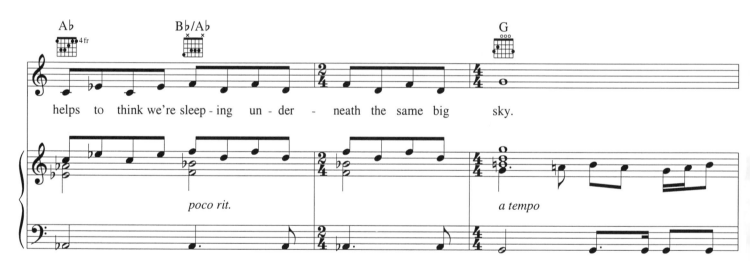

when the night _ wind starts to sing a lone - some lull - a - by it

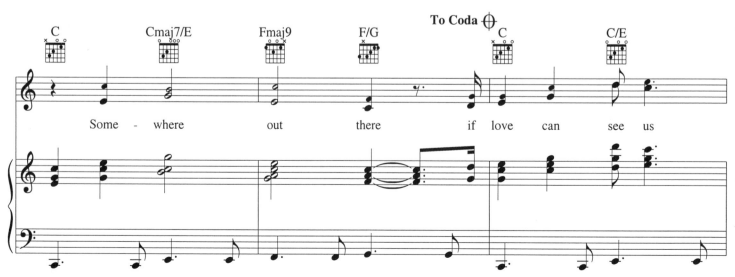

helps to think we're sleep - ing un - der - neath the same big sky.

poco rit. *a tempo*

Some - where out there if love can see us

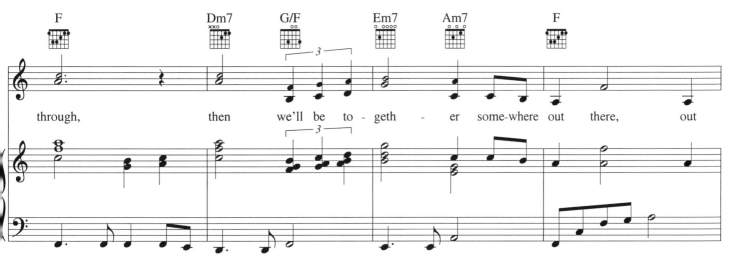

through, then we'll be to - geth - er some-where out there, out

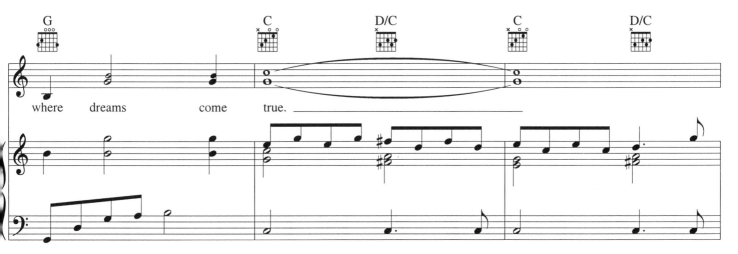

where dreams come true. _____

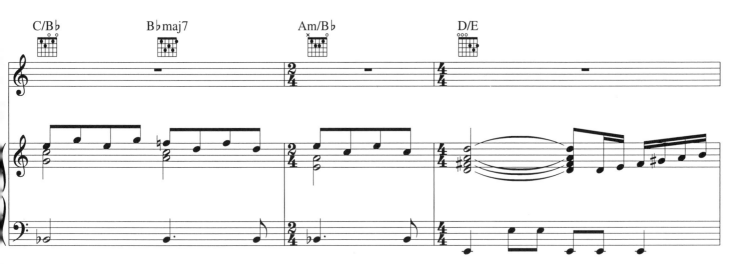

Still

Words and Music by
LIONEL RICHIE

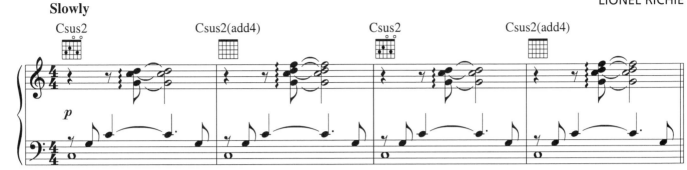

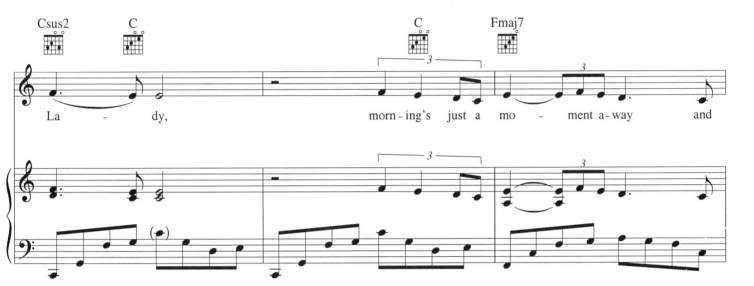

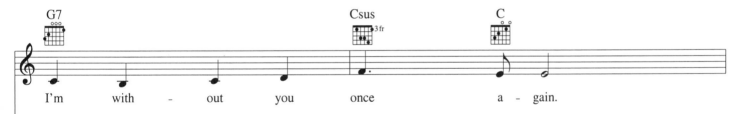

you said you've nev-er need-ed __ me; I

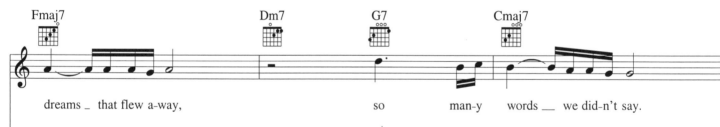

won - der if you need me now. So man-y __

dreams _ that flew a-way, so man-y words __ we did-n't say.

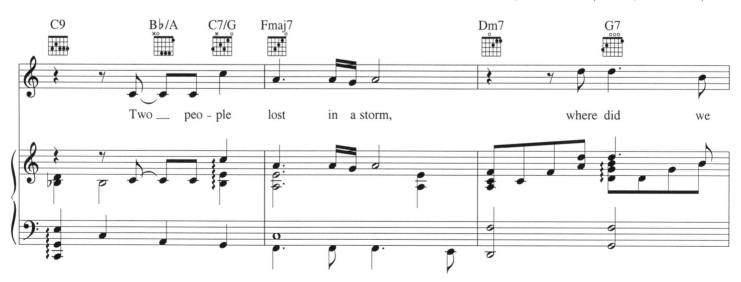

Two __ peo-ple lost in a storm, where did we

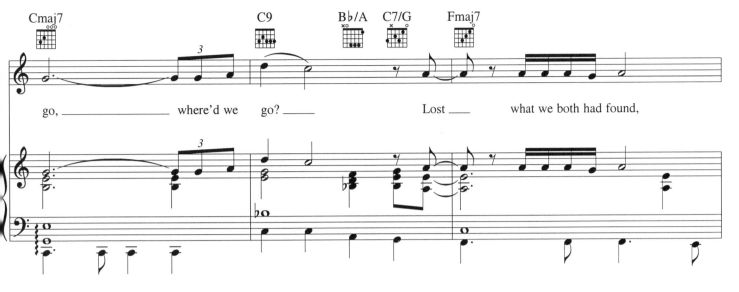

go, _____ where'd we go? _____ Lost ___ what we both had found,

you know we let _____ each oth - er down.

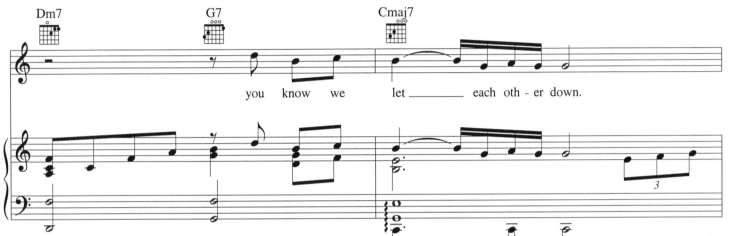

But then ___ most of all   I do love ___ you

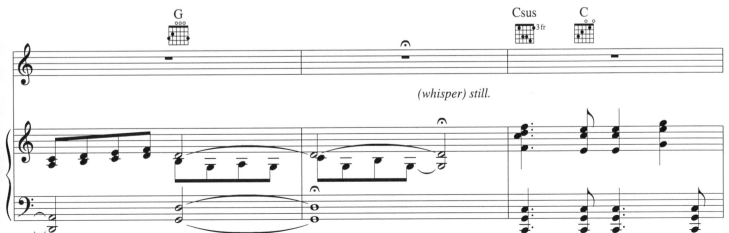

(whisper) still.

Strangers in the Night
adapted from A MAN COULD GET KILLED

Words by CHARLES SINGLETON and EDDIE SNYDER
Music by BERT KAEMPFERT

Stran- gers in the night _____ ex- chang- ing glanc - es,

won-d'ring in the night _____ what were the chanc - es we'd be shar- ing love _____

_ be- fore the night was through. _____ Some-thing in your eyes _____

MCA Music Publishing

Tears in Heaven

Words and Music by ERIC CLAPTON
and WILL JENNINGS

Be-yond   the   door ___   there's peace,   I'm   sure, _

Three Times a Lady

Words and Music by
LIONEL RICHIE

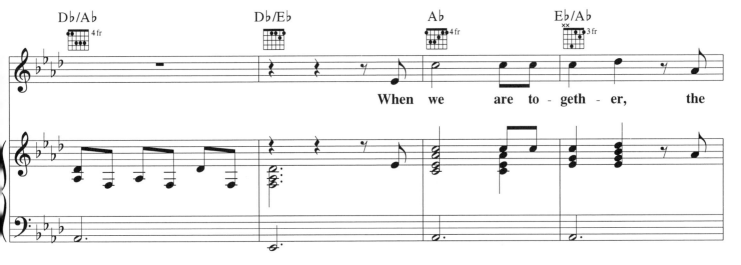

When we are to-geth-er, the

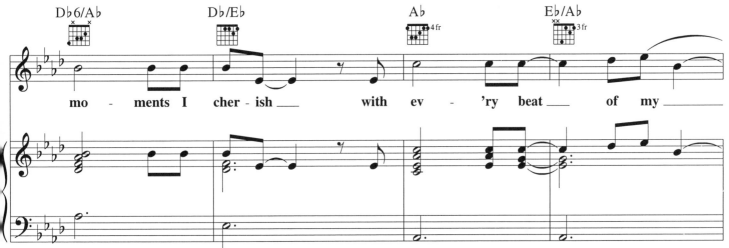

mo-ments I cher-ish ___ with ev-'ry beat ___ of my ___

___ heart; ___ To touch you, to hold you, to

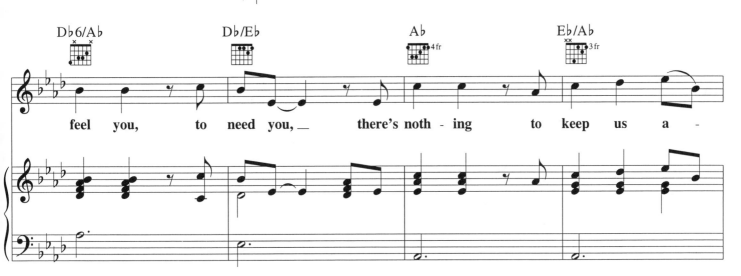

feel you, to need you, ___ there's noth-ing to keep us a -

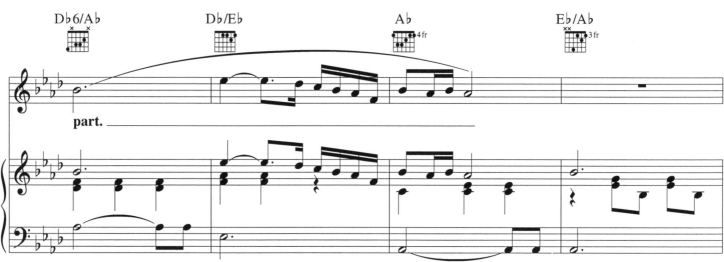

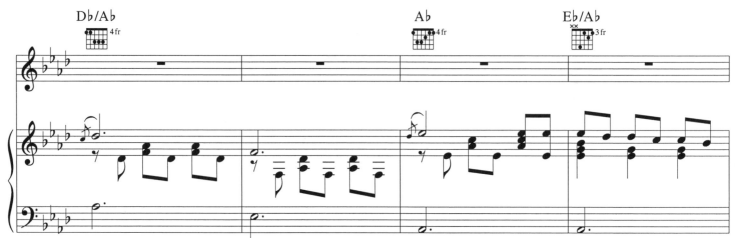

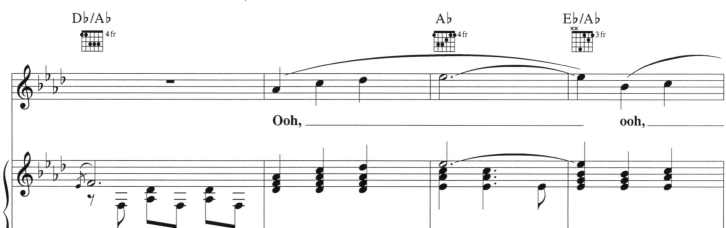

With pedal

Unchained Melody
featured in the Motion Picture GHOST

Lyric by HY ZARET
Music by ALEX NORTH

Moderately slow

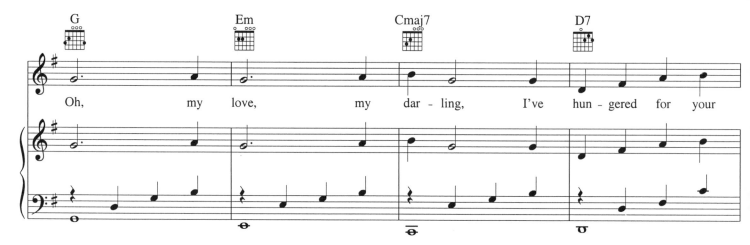

Oh, my love, my dar-ling, I've hun-gered for your touch a long, lone-ly time. ___

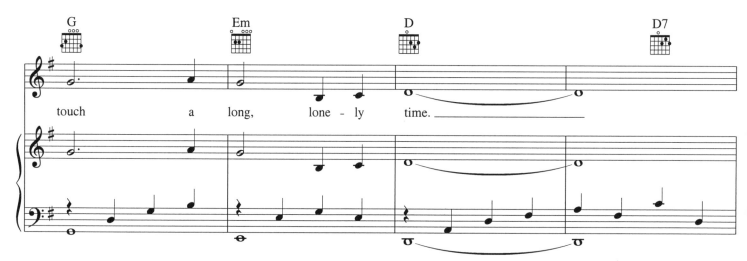

Time goes by so slow-ly and time can do so

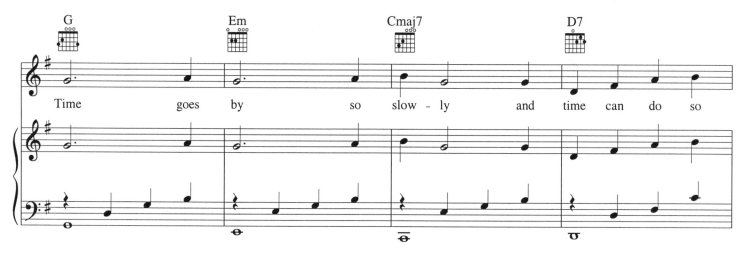

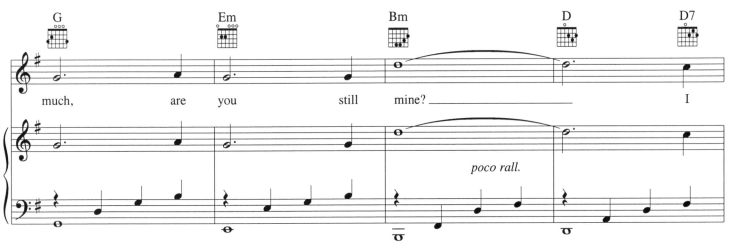

much, are you still mine? _____ I

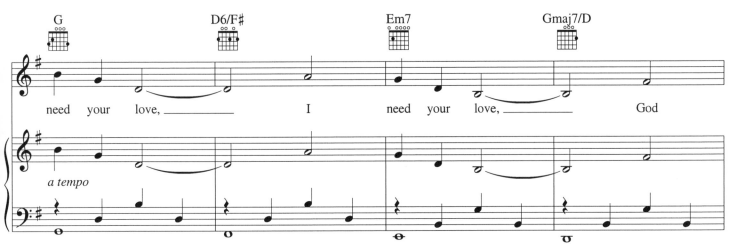

need your love, _____ I need your love, _____ God

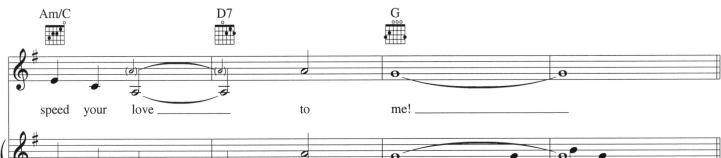

speed your love _____ to me! _____

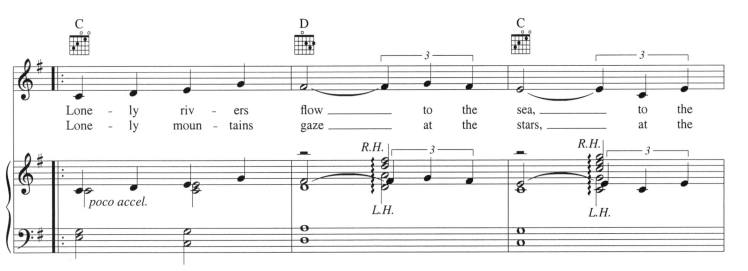

Lone - ly riv - ers flow _____ to the sea, _____ to the
Lone - ly moun - tains gaze _____ at the stars, _____ at the

Tempo I

Oh, my love, my dar - ling, I've

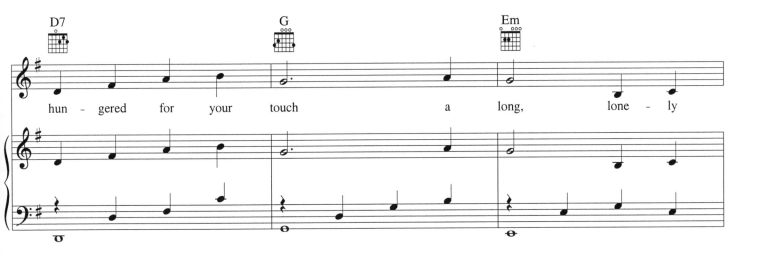

hun - gered for your touch a long, lone - ly

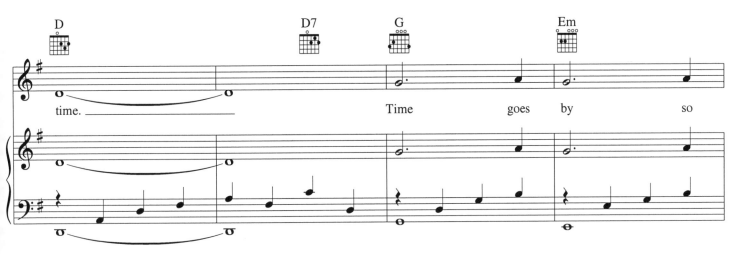

time. _____ Time goes by so

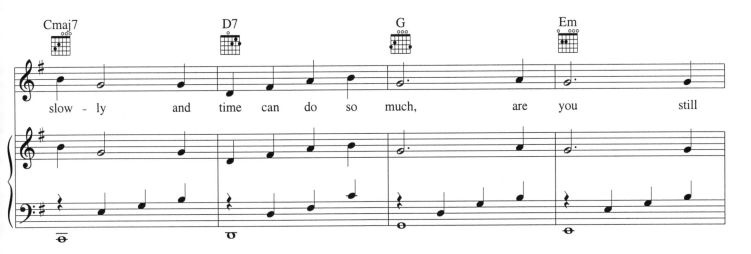

slow - ly and time can do so much, are you still

Uninvited
from the Motion Picture CITY OF ANGELS

Words and Music by
ALANIS MORISSETTE

MCA Music Publishing

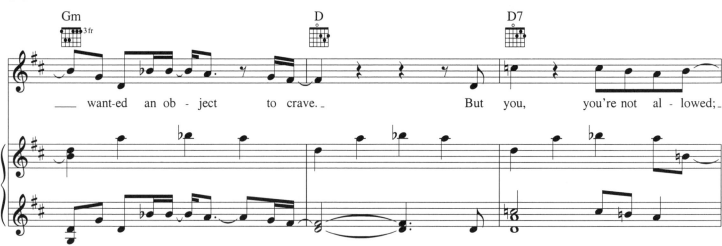

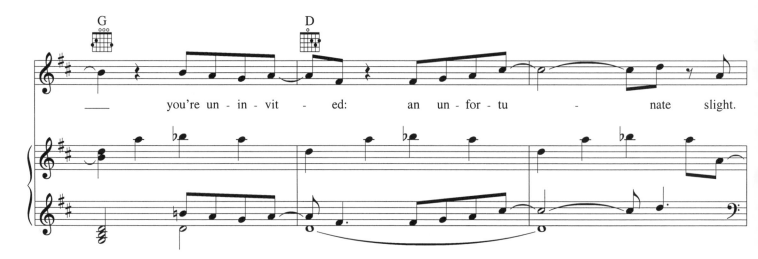

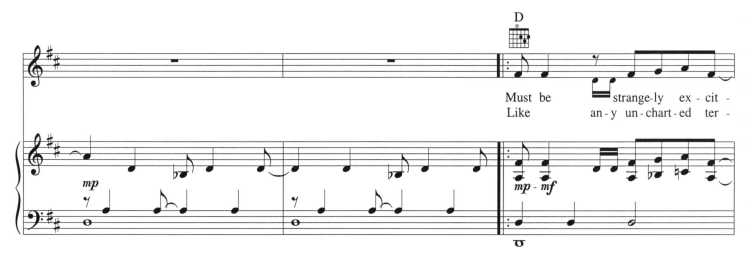

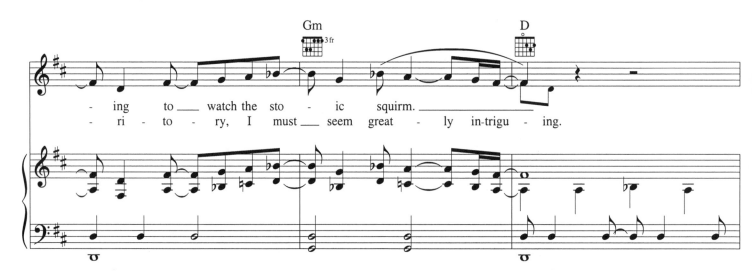

I don't think you un-wor - thy; I need a mo-

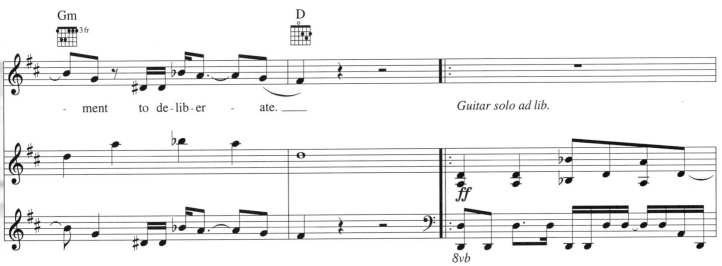

Gm   D

- ment to de-lib-er - ate. _____   *Guitar solo ad lib.*

Play 4 times   D5

Valentine

Words and Music by JACK KUGELL
and JIM BRICKMAN

Smoothly

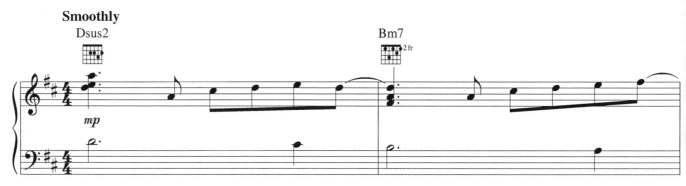

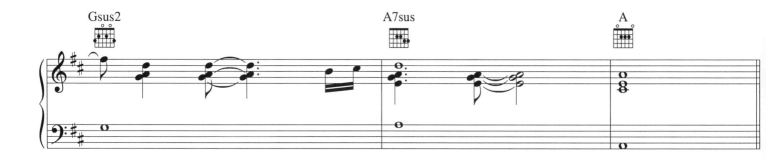

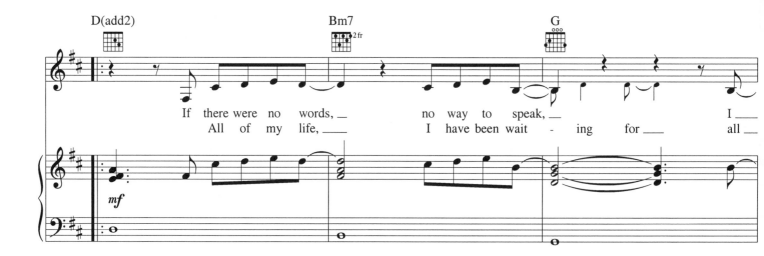

If there were no words, __ no way to speak, __ I
All of my life, __ I have been wait - ing for __ all

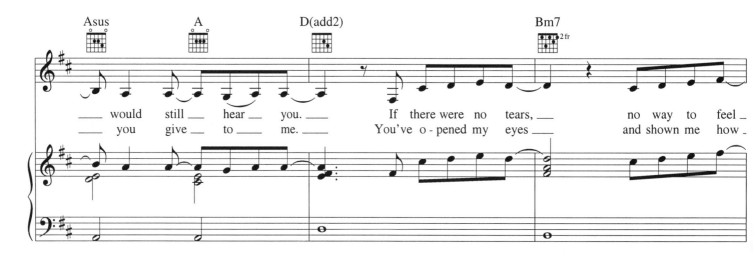

__ would still __ hear __ you. __ If there were no tears, __ no way to feel __
__ you give to __ me. __ You've o - pened my eyes __ and shown me how __

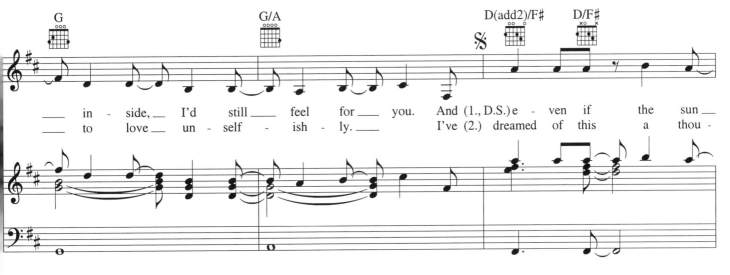

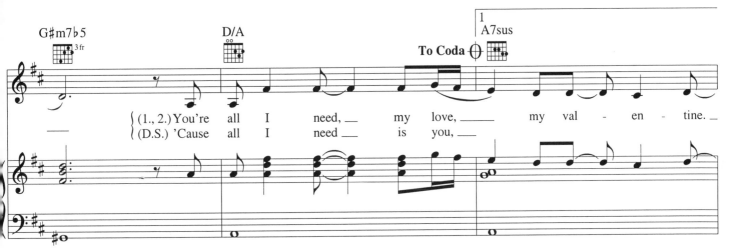

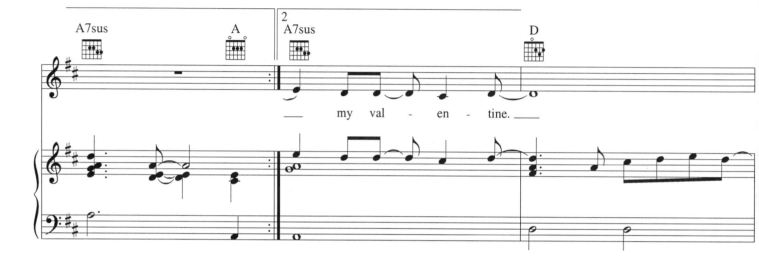

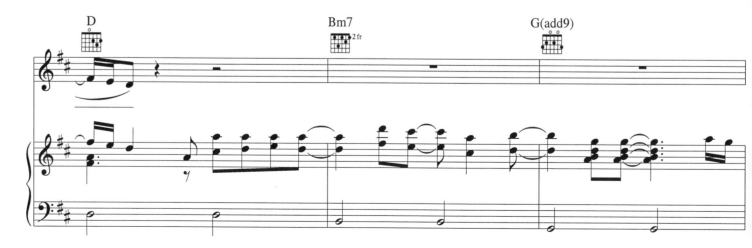

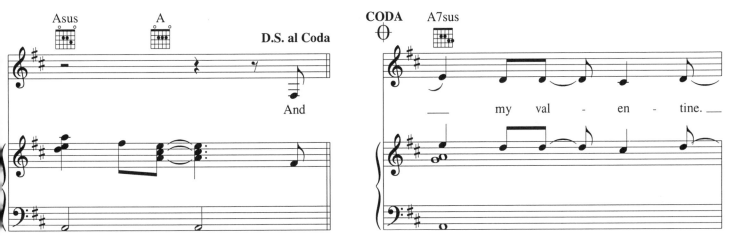

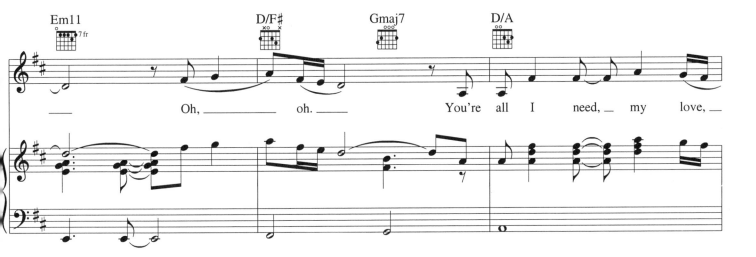

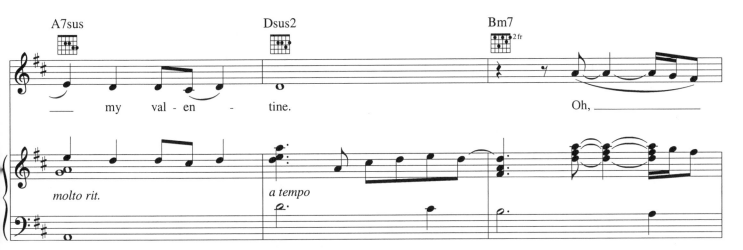

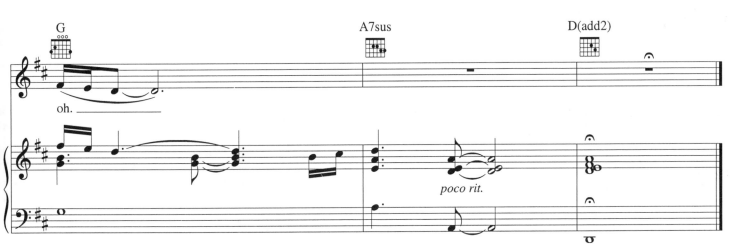

The Way You Look Tonight
from SWING TIME

Words by DOROTHY FIELDS
Music by JEROME KERN

When I Fall in Love

featured in the TriStar Motion Picture SLEEPLESS IN SEATTLE

Words by EDWARD HEYMAN
Music by VICTOR YOUNG

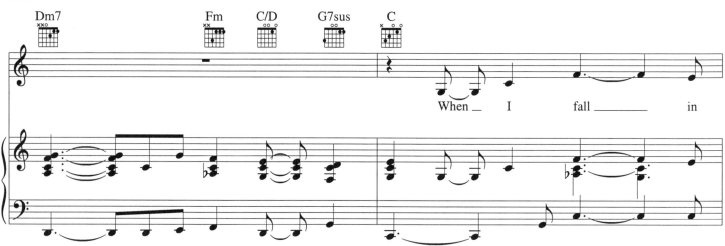

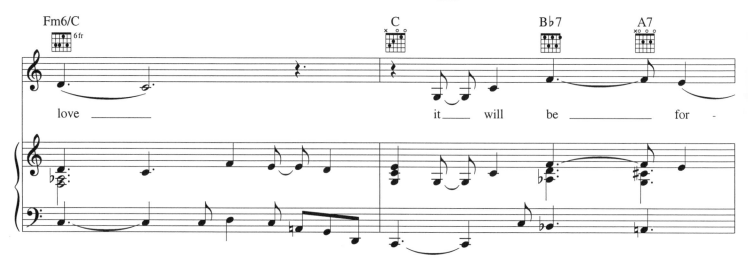

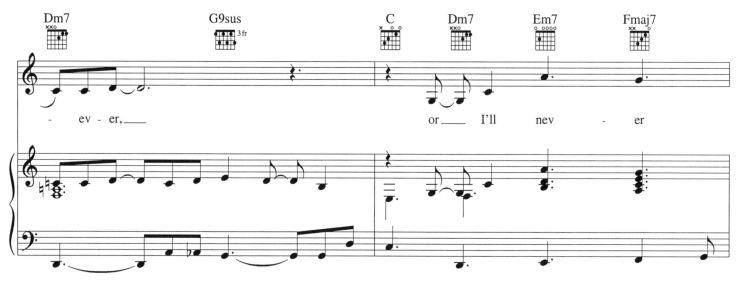

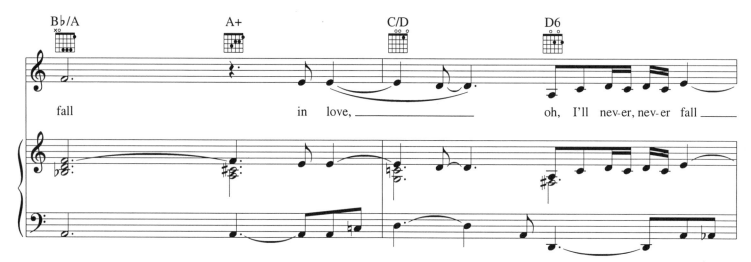

in love. _____ In ___ a rest - less world ___ like

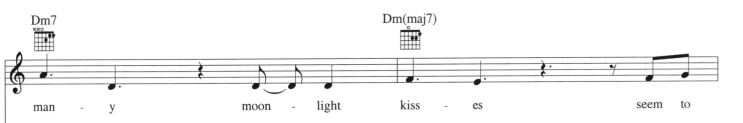

this is, ___ love is end - ed ___ be - fore it's ___ be - gun, and too

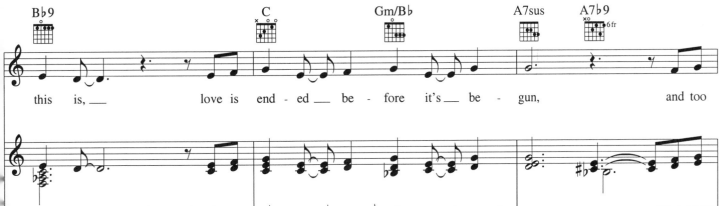

man - y moon - light kiss - es seem to

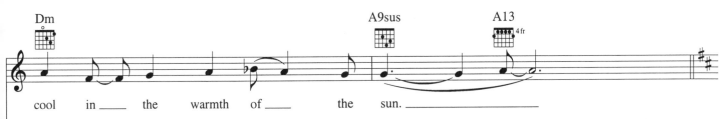

cool in ___ the warmth of ___ the sun. _____

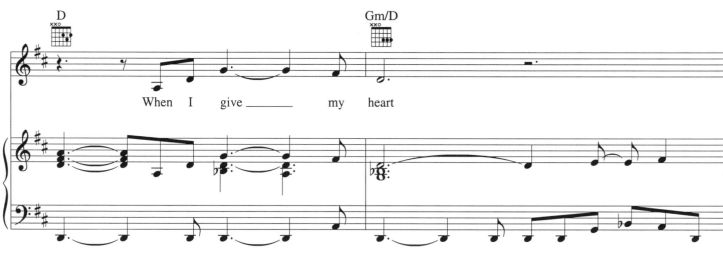

When I give _____ my heart

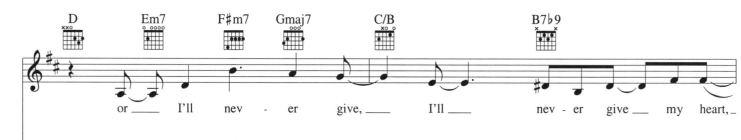

it will be _____ com - plete - ly, ___

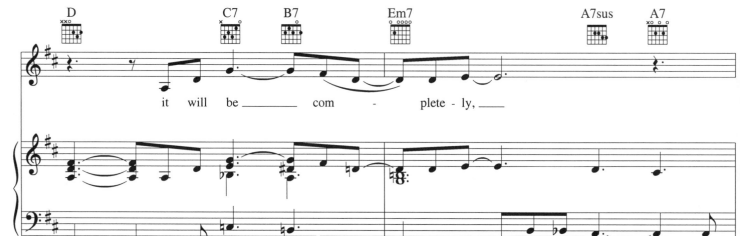

or ___ I'll nev - er give, ___ I'll ___ nev - er give ___ my heart, _

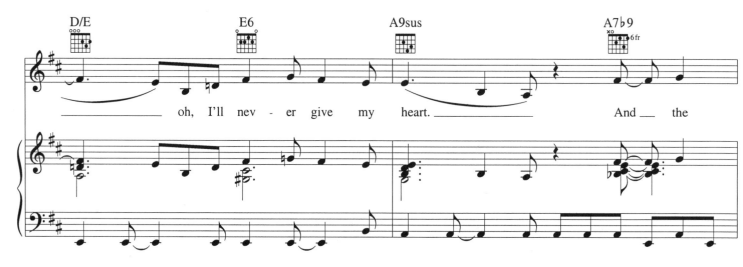

_____ oh, I'll nev - er give my heart. _____ And __ the

What a Wonderful World

Words and Music by GEORGE DAVID WEISS
and BOB THIELE

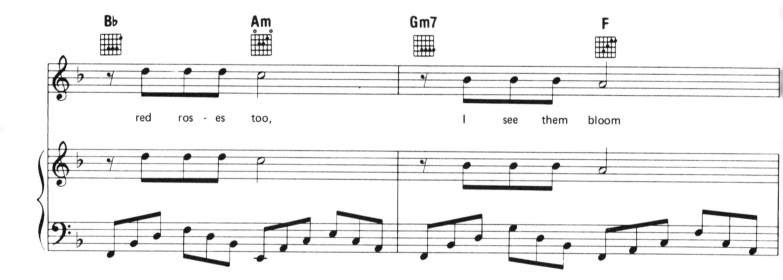

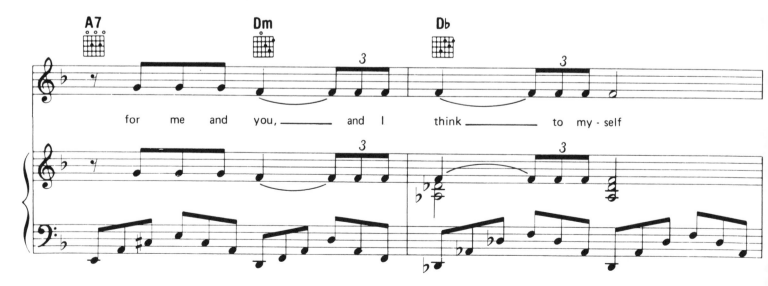

col - ors of the rain - bow, so pret - ty in the sky are

al - so on the fac - es of peo - ple go - in' by, I see

friends shak - in' hands, _____ say - in', "How do you do!"

They're real - ly say - in' "I love you," I hear

When You Say Nothing at All

Words and Music by DON SCHLITZ
and PAUL OVERSTREET

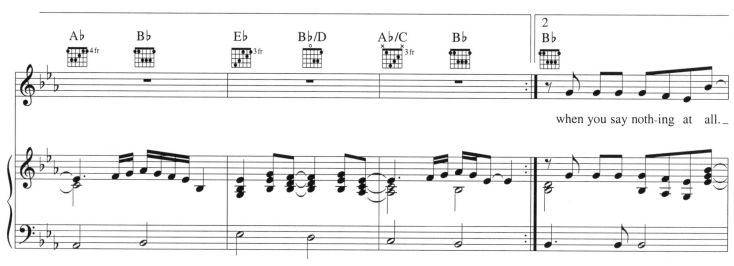

when you say noth-ing at all. _

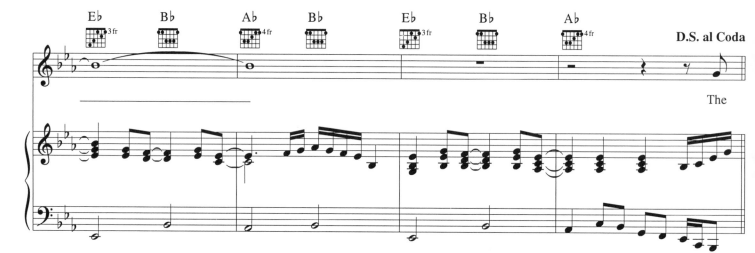

D.S. al Coda

The

CODA

when you say noth-ing at all. _____

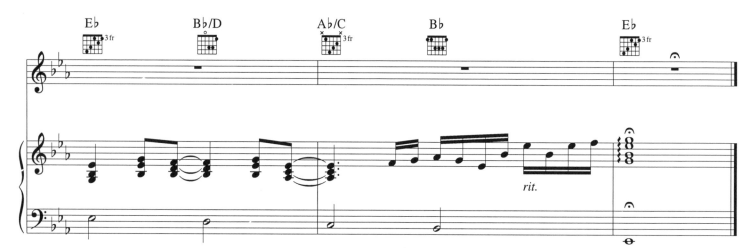

rit.

Yester-Me, Yester-You, Yesterday

Words by RON MILLER
Music by BRYAN WELLS

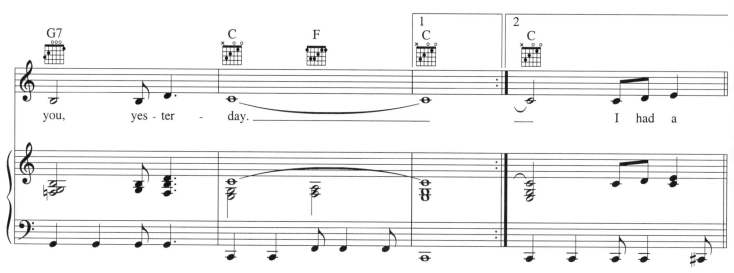

you, yes - ter - day. _____ I had a

dream, so did you. Life was warm, love was
call what we had, I feel

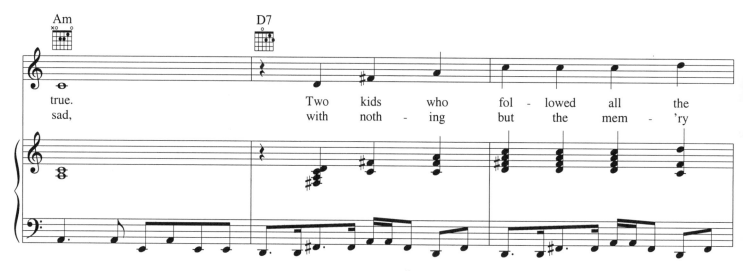

true. Two kids who fol - lowed all the
sad, with noth - ing but the all mem - 'ry

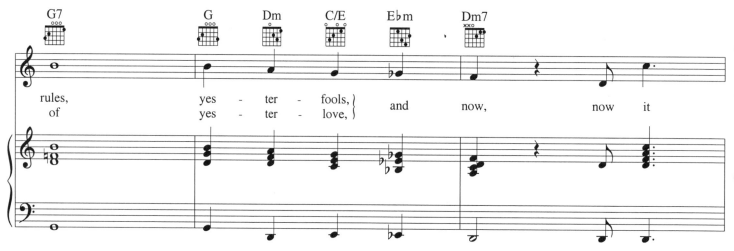

rules, yes - ter - fools,
of yes - ter - love, and now, now it

seems _____ those yes - ter - dreams

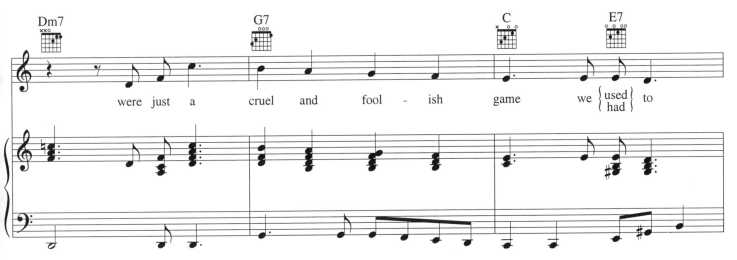

were just a cruel and fool - ish game we {used}{had} to

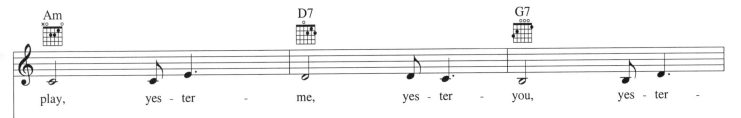

play, yes - ter - me, yes - ter - you, yes - ter -

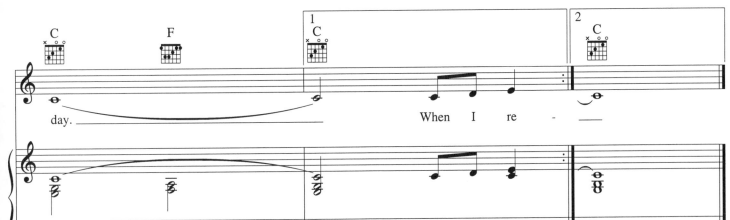

day. _____ When I re - ___

A Whole New World
(Aladdin's Theme)
from Walt Disney's ALADDIN
As Performed by Peabo Bryson and Regina Belle

Music by ALAN MENKEN
Lyrics by TIM RICE

Wonderful Tonight

Words and Music by
ERIC CLAPTON

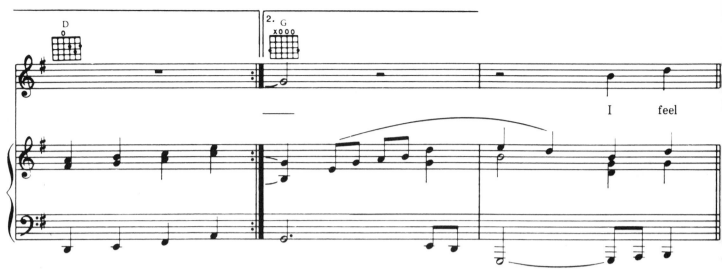

277

You and I

Words and Music by
STEVIE WONDER

Slowly, with feeling

Here we are on earth to-geth-er it's you and I.
I am glad at least in my life I found some-one

God __ has made __ us fall in __ love, it's true. __
that may not be here for-ev-er to see me through. __

I've
But

real-ly found __ some-one like you.
I found strength __ in __ you.

I

in my mind __ we can con - quer the world.
in my mind __ you will stay here al - ways.

In love, you and I. You and I. You and
In love, you and I. You and I. You and

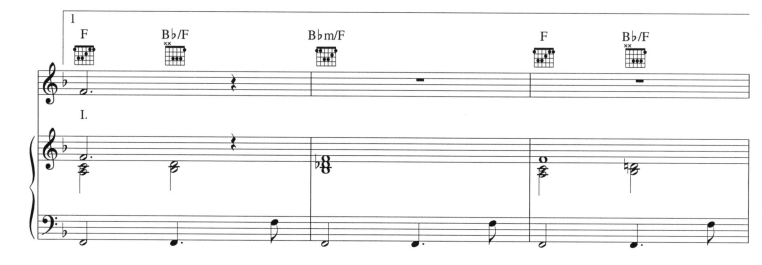

1
I.

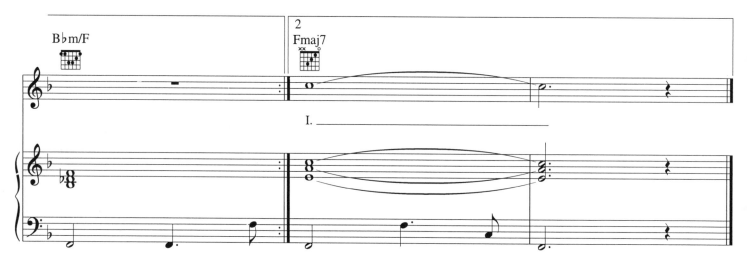

2

I.

You Must Love Me
from the Cinergi Motion Picture EVITA

Words by TIM RICE
Music by ANDREW LLOYD WEBBER

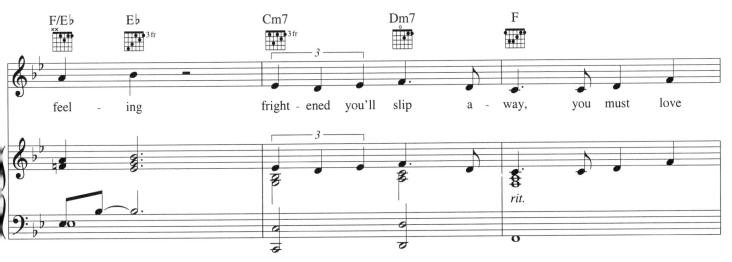

feel - ing   fright - ened you'll slip   a - way,   you must   love

me,   you must   love   me.

You   must   love   me.

Additional Lyrics

Verse 2: *(Instrumental 8 bars)*
Why are you at my side?
How can I be any use to you now?
Give me a chance and I'll let you see how
Nothing has changed.
Deep in my heart I'm concealing
Things that I'm longing to say,
Scared to confess what I'm feeling
Frightened you'll slip away,
You must love me.

You've Got a Friend

Words and Music by
CAROLE KING

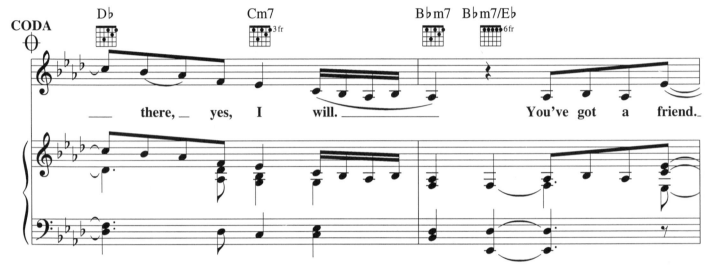

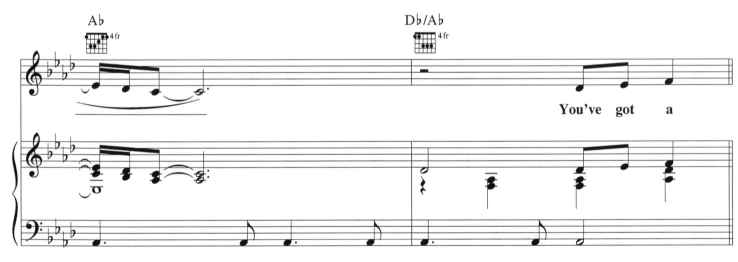